Marian Cox

Cambridge Checkpoint
English
Coursebook
7

CAMBRIDGE
UNIVERSITY PRESS

CAMBRIDGE
UNIVERSITY PRESS

University Printing House, Cambridge CB2 8BS, United Kingdom

One Liberty Plaza, 20th Floor, New York, NY 10006, USA

477 Williamstown Road, Port Melbourne, VIC 3207, Australia

314–321, 3rd Floor, Plot 3, Splendor Forum, Jasola District Centre, New Delhi – 110025, India

79 Anson Road, #06–04/06, Singapore 079906

Cambridge University Press is part of the University of Cambridge.

It furthers the University's mission by disseminating knowledge in the pursuit of education, learning and research at the highest international levels of excellence.

www.cambridge.org
Information on this title: www.cambridge.org/9781107670235

© Cambridge University Press 2012

This publication is in copyright. Subject to statutory exception and to the provisions of relevant collective licensing agreements, no reproduction of any part may take place without the written permission of Cambridge University Press.

First published 2012

20

Printed in India by Repro India Ltd

A catalogue record for this publication is available from the British Library

ISBN 978-1-107-67023-5 Paperback

Cambridge University Press has no responsibility for the persistence or accuracy of URLs for external or third-party internet websites referred to in this publication, and does not guarantee that any content on such websites is, or will remain, accurate or appropriate.

Contents

Introduction — iv

Unit 1 House and home — 1
acrostic poem; autobiography; informal letter; proverb; fable

Unit 2 Tall tales — 13
cautionary tale; urban legend; mini-saga; horror/suspense story

Unit 3 Favourite things — 25
song lyric; discursive text; recipe; menu; descriptive poetry; personal account

Unit 4 School stories — 40
first-person narrative; figurative description; poem; semi-formal letter; diary

Unit 5 Up in the air — 54
informative text; news report; advertisement; novel extracts; legend; talk

Unit 6 Imaginary worlds — 69
fairy tale; plot synopsis; blurb; book review; fantasy/sci-fi story

Unit 7 Down to earth — 83
magazine article; shape poem; autobiography; descriptive poem; novel extract; descriptive prose

Unit 8 Hidden treasure — 95
plot synopsis; playscript; story continuation; quest story

Unit 9 Meet the family — 109
monologue; personal account; fact list; news feature; lyrical poetry

Unit 10 Mysteries and puzzles — 125
short story extract; ballad extract; narrative poem; factual account; mystery story

Unit 11 Looking back — 135
memoirs; nostalgia poems; lyrical poem; rhythm poem; confession letters

Unit 12 Secret lives — 153
fantasy novel extracts; fantasy poems; horror novel extract; song lyric

Acknowledgements — 164

Introduction

Welcome to Cambridge Checkpoint English Stage 7.

The Cambridge Checkpoint English course covers the Cambridge Secondary 1 English framework and is divided into three stages: 7, 8 and 9. This book covers all you need to know for stage 7.

There are two more books in the series to cover stages 8 and 9, which have a different focus. Together they will give you a firm foundation in English across a full range of language and literature skills.

At the end of the year, your teacher may ask you to take a **Progression test** to find out how well you have done. This book will help you to learn how to apply your knowledge of language and your skills in reading and writing in order to do well in the test. At the end of stage 9, you will be asked to do a **Checkpoint test** to find out how much you have learnt over all three stages.

The framework's focus for stage 7 is **Narration and reflection**. The curriculum is divided into Reading, Writing, and Speaking and Listening. From 2018, Language Usage is assessed within Writing. There is no assessment of Speaking and Listening in the Progression tests or the Checkpoint test, but these essential skills, practised as individual, pair, group and class activities, are developed in all the units, as they are an important part of increasing your understanding of language and literature.

The topic for this book is **My world**. The content is about home and school, family and friends.

This book has 12 units, half of which are focused mostly on fiction, and half on non-fiction. There are no clear dividing lines between fiction and non-fiction texts, language and literature, or between reading and writing skills. Skills learned in one unit are often used in other units. There is, however, some progression in the order in which the skills are introduced.

Each unit starts with an introduction which will prepare you for what you will learn in the unit, and a starter activity to get you thinking and talking. You will then read several kinds of passage and be asked to practise various skills. **Key points** explain rules and give information about aspects of reading and writing, and **Tip** boxes provide help with specific activities. The activities are separated into stages to give you support. At the end of each unit you will be asked to do a piece of extended writing to give you the opportunity to practise the kind of writing you will be asked to do in the Checkpoint test. Other kinds of writing will be included in the activities. You will also practise reading the kinds of passage which are included in the Checkpoint test, and learn to read closely so that you notice the details of the content and of the language of what you read.

There are many different types of verse and prose in this book, and your knowledge and understanding of literature will be developed as well as your language skills. The contents list on page iii tells you what kinds of reading passage and writing activities are in each unit.

We hope the course will be enjoyable and will help you to feel confident about responding to and using English in a variety of ways.

UNIT 1 House and home

This unit focuses on your house and home environment, and on autobiographical writing. You will practise skimming and scanning, giving instructions and directions, defining words and ideas, and making imaginative comparisons. You will revise parts of speech and sentence separation, and look at some difficult spellings.

Activities

1
  a Write down five words or phrases which come into your mind when you think of the word *home*.

  b How many homes have you lived in? Think of the homes you have had, and write down words to describe what they were like.

  c Talk briefly in small groups about what is important about having a home. In your group, after everyone has contributed to the discussion, make a list of the ideas you have talked about. Report your ideas back to the class.

Text 1A

An acrostic poem

H aven from the noisy world
O pen door to my sanctuary
M akes me feel safe and snug
E ven when I am sad

2
  a Look carefully at the layout of the poem in Text 1A. Can you define an acrostic poem?

  b Write three acrostic poems of your own using the word *H O M E*. Try to use images, or figurative language, as in the poem in Text 1A. Look at the key point on figurative language on page 2 to help you.

  c Ask your partner which one they like best and why.

Cambridge Checkpoint English 7

Key point

Figurative language

Figurative language refers to words that are used not in a strictly factual way but to make imaginative comparisons between one idea and another. In Text 1A, for example, the words *haven* (a protected place for boats) and *sanctuary* (safety in a religious building) are being used as an image, in this case as a metaphor. A comparison introduced by *as* or *like* is called a simile, as in *My home is like a warm nest*.

3 The ten words below are the names of different types of places people live in. For each of the places in the list, write a definition which describes it exactly. You may need to use a dictionary for some of them. Keep your answers as brief as possible, and make sure that they are all clear and different from each other.

bungalow	caravan/trailer	cottage	flat/apartment	mansion
palace	penthouse	tent	villa	yurt

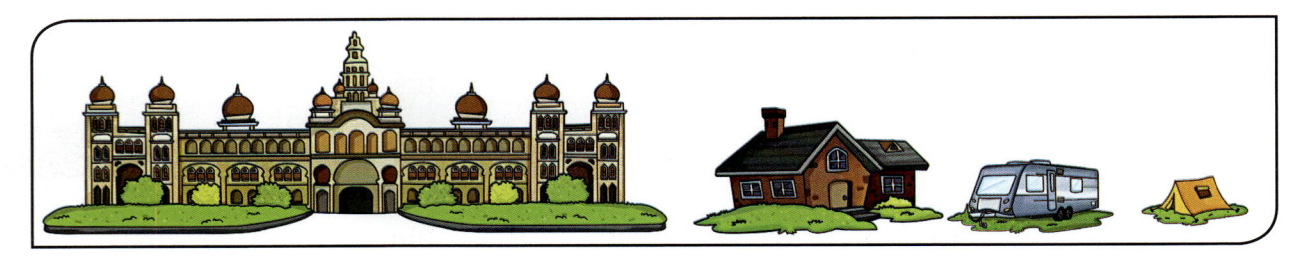

Key point

Giving instructions and directions

Giving an instruction or direction is a bit like giving a short, clear definition of a word. It is an important skill. Clear instructions enable people to follow what we want them to do or what they need to do without getting confused or lost. The important thing when giving instructions is to be very clear and precise.

- We use imperative (command) verb forms, such as 'Take the first . . .' or 'Turn right at . . .'
- The stages must always be in the right order, and we keep them brief and separate by using short sentences or bullet points.
- Words must be chosen carefully so that no misunderstanding is possible.

UNIT 1 House and home

4 **a** Give directions for a journey you know well, such as how to get from your house to your school. Use the tip below to help you.

  b Draw a simple map showing your house in its garden and surroundings: the neighbouring houses, streets, shops, parks and any other features of the area.

  c Label your map, using brief and precise definitions, such as 'My brother's school', 'Main road to centre of town', 'The Jolly Café'.

> **Tip**
>
> **For Activity 4a**
> **Using reference points in directions**
>
> Traffic lights, crossroads, roundabouts and other road junctions are the usual reference points when giving directions. Sometimes prominent features of the landscape are also referred to, like tall buildings, shops and signs, bridges and parks. We might say, for example, 'When you have passed the supermarket on the left, take the next turn on the right' or 'Turn right just before the bridge'. You can use a noticeable feature of your house to tell someone how they will know when they have arrived. For example, 'My house is the one with the red front door and the swing in the garden.'

5 **a** How would you describe your house? List adjectives and phrases which give a picture of the size, shape, style, colours and appearance of the <u>outside</u> of your house, for example 'brick-built', 'flat-roofed'.

  b Think of interesting features of particular rooms <u>inside</u> your house, and how you can describe them. Things to consider are:
  - shapes
  - furniture
  - decorations
  - colour schemes
  - atmosphere
  - views from the windows
  - what the rooms are used for.

  c Imagine you have a new penfriend in another country who wants to know all about where you live. Write a letter or email to your penfriend describing your home and neighbourhood. Use the tip on page 4 and the key point about informal letters to help you.

Tip

For Activity 5c
Describing your home and neighbourhood

You could start with a description of the inside of your house and then talk about the outside, the garden, the street and finally the area, or you could start with the area and work back to the inside of the house. The important thing is to have some kind of logical order in your description, rather than jumping between inside and outside. Add details for interest, and say what you like and dislike about where you live, so that you are reflecting and sharing your thoughts as well as just giving factual information.

Key point

Informal letters

When you write to someone you know, or who is your age, in a letter, email or blog, you can use informal, everyday English, although it's a good idea to use correct spelling and grammar so that there is no problem with understanding. Even though you are being casual, if your letter has some order and the ideas are connected, it helps the reader follow what you are saying.

6 Look at the five proverbs about home below. Have you heard of any of them? Working in pairs, try and think of other famous sayings that include the word *home* or *house*.

1 Home Sweet Home
2 Home is where the heart is.
3 There's no place like home.
4 A house is not a home.
5 East, west, home's best.

UNIT 1 House and home

Key point

Proverbs

Proverbs are anonymous famous sayings which concisely explain a commonly held belief within a culture. Many beliefs exist across cultures but are expressed using a different image. For example, the proverb 'A bird in the hand is worth two in the bush', which is well known in the UK and the USA, is expressed in China as 'Distant water won't help to put out a fire close at hand'.

Proverbs are often metaphors. A metaphor is a memorable way of comparing two things or ideas by suggesting, but not actually stating, that they are similar. Recognising figurative language of all kinds, including proverbs, in what you read will help you understand how writers create effects. It will also help you become a writer yourself.

7 a With your partner, decide how to paraphrase, i.e. rewrite in your own words, the proverbs in Activity 6 so that their meaning is clear.

b Now choose one of the proverbs as the title for a very short story to explain the meaning of the proverb. Think of a character and an event to include in your story. Use the tip below to help you.

c Write your story, which should be about half a page. You could read your story to the class and listen to how other students have used the same proverb in a different way.

Tip

For Activity 7b
Illustrating a proverb

A story which explains a proverb is a kind of fable, which means a story with a moral, or a lesson to be learned. You can illustrate the moral by writing about what happens to the character in your story. Show how their particular experience changes their understanding. Often the characters in fables are animals to represent universal human types. You could include a conclusion which sums up the proverb; a separate summing up of the moral at the end of the story is sometimes found in fables, as in *Aesop's Fables*.

Stolen food

This passage is an extract from Helen Keller's autobiography, *The Story of My Life*. An autobiography is someone's life story written by that person. Helen Keller was born in 1880 in the USA. She lost her sight and hearing in an illness when she was two years old. Note that the spelling in this extract is American.

I do not remember when I first realized that I was different from other people, but I knew it before my teacher came to me. I had noticed that my mother and my friends did not use signs as I did when they wanted anything done, but talked with their mouths. Sometimes I stood between two persons who were conversing and touched their lips. I could not understand, <u>and</u> was vexed. I moved my lips <u>and</u> **gesticulated** frantically without result. This made me so angry at times that I kicked and screamed until I was exhausted.

I think I knew when I was naughty, for I knew that it hurt Ella, my nurse, to kick her, <u>and</u> when my fit of temper was over I had a feeling akin to regret. But I cannot remember any instance in which this feeling prevented me from repeating the naughtiness when I failed to get what I wanted.

In those days, Martha Washington, the child of our cook, and Belle, an old hound, and a great hunter in her day, were my constant companions. Martha Washington understood my signs, <u>and</u> I seldom had any difficulty in making her do just as I wished. It pleased me to **domineer** over her, <u>and</u> she generally submitted to my **tyranny** rather than risk a hand-to-hand **encounter**. I was strong, active, indifferent to consequences. I knew my own mind well enough <u>and</u> always had my own way, even if I had to fight tooth and nail for it. We spent a great deal of time in the kitchen, kneading dough balls, helping make ice-cream, grinding coffee, quarreling over the cake-bowl, and feeding the hens and turkeys that swarmed about the kitchen steps. Many of them were so tame that they would eat from my hand <u>and</u> let me feel them. One big gobbler snatched a tomato from me one day <u>and</u> ran away with it. Inspired, perhaps, by Master Gobbler's success, we carried off to the woodpile a cake which the cook had just frosted, <u>and</u> ate every bit of it. I was quite ill afterward, <u>and</u> I wondered if **retribution** also overtook the turkey.

UNIT 1 House and home

In the next four activities, you will be looking at the language used in Text 1B, and exploring its vocabulary and grammar.

8 a Read Text 1B, then use a dictionary to find the meanings of the five words in bold in the passage.

b Give the part of speech (noun, verb, adjective, and so on) for each of the words in bold, as used in the passage.

c The word *and* can be used to link two equal items, as in 'my mother and my friends'. The underlined *and*s in Text 1B are being used for a different purpose, though – to make compound sentences. Look again at the sentences with *and* in Text 1B. Can you say what a compound sentence is, and what would happen if the *and* was removed from this sort of sentence?

9 It helps spelling accuracy to recognise letter strings and silent letters. Work with a partner and list:
- words containing *gn* where the *g* is silent, as in 'sign' in Text 1B
- words beginning with *kn* where the *k* is silent, as in 'kneading' in the passage
- words containing *qu*, which is a fixed letter string in English, as in 'consequences' in the passage.

10 a There are figurative or metaphorical uses of language in Text 1B (things said which are exaggerated or not actually true), for example 'big gobbler'. Work with a partner to find as many of the figurative uses of language as you can. Underline them on a copy of the passage.

b Write definitions of the literal (actual) meanings of the figurative expressions you have found.

c Discuss as a class how the figurative words or phrases make the idea behind them stronger and more memorable than the literal meanings.

11 a On your copy of Text 1B, find and underline the words which tell us about Helen's character.

b Describe in single words and phrases of your own the personality of Helen Keller.

c Which references and words in the passage show that, although an adult is writing it, the reader is being given the viewpoint of a child?

Cambridge Checkpoint English 7

Key point

Reader viewpoint

Writers position or manipulate the reader to like or dislike characters by revealing things about them which are attractive or unattractive, and by using language which invites either sympathy or disapproval. In first-person narratives (using *I*) the reader is also given a particular viewpoint by the narrator, so that the reader can understand how the narrator looks at things and feels about them, and this helps the reader to identify with the narrator. For instance, the narrator may be pretending to be a child again, or to be unaware of what is really happening. You can tell by the kind of language they use and the things they talk about how grown-up they are. Another way of suggesting a child's viewpoint is to make everything seem big and frightening because the child is small by comparison.

Text 1C

Arriving at a new home

This passage, from the beginning of another autobiography, is about the feelings of a young boy whose family moves from the town to the country.

I was set down from the carrier's cart at the age of three; and there with a sense of bewilderment and terror my life in the village began. The June grass, amongst which I stood, was taller than I was, and I wept. I had never been so close to grass before. It towered above me and all around me, *each blade tattooed with tiger-skins of sunlight*. It was *knife-edged, dark, and a wicked green,* thick as a forest and alive with grasshoppers that chirped and chattered and leapt through the air like monkeys. I was lost and didn't know where to move. *A tropic heat oozed up* from the ground, rank with sharp odours of roots and nettles. Snow-clouds of elder blossom banked in the sky, showering upon me the *fumes and flakes* of their *sweet and giddy suffocation*. High overhead ran frenzied larks, screaming, as though the sky were tearing apart. For the first time in my life I was out of the sight of humans. For the first time in my life I was alone in a world whose behaviour I could neither predict nor fathom: a world of birds that squealed, of plants that stank, of insects that sprang about without warning. I was lost and I did not expect to be found again. I put back my head and howled, and the sun hit me smartly on the face, like a bully.

From Cider with Rosie *by Laurie Lee*

UNIT 1 House and home

Key point

Skimming and scanning

When you first read a passage which you know you will have to answer questions on, it's a good idea to skim it quickly to get a sense of what it is about, to grasp the gist of it. It is useful, before getting down to details, to have a general understanding of the kind of writing it is, and to be able to answer the questions *Who? What? When? Where? Why?* At this stage you also need to notice which words you don't know the meaning of, so that you can look them up in a dictionary or ask someone.

When you are clear about the content of the passage and the meaning of all the words, then you are ready to look at the question, followed by a re-reading of the passage. The second time you read you should scan for the information needed to answer the question, and underline the relevant ideas when you find them.

12
a Skim read Text 1C. Then write, in one sentence, a summary of the situation in the passage.

b Now scan the passage, selecting the words and phrases that you think show how small and vulnerable the child feels.

c Using your own words, explain the five metaphors which are in italics in the passage.

13 This activity will help you explore the structure of the sentences in Text 1C. First, look back at Activity 8c and remind yourself of the different uses of *and* that you came across in Text 1B.

a Now look at Text 1C. Can you find five examples in Text 1C of *and* being used as a connective between clauses (groups of words containing a main verb) to make compound sentences?

b We could replace these uses of *and* with a full stop and a pronoun (e.g. *He, She, It*) to begin the next sentence. Try it out for yourself and then say how you think it makes a difference to the passage to change compound sentences into simple sentences.

c Text 1D on the next page is the next paragraph of the passage in Text 1C. Read Text 1D and look carefully at the use of full stops. Discuss in pairs why you think full stops must be used in these places.

Cambridge Checkpoint English 7

Text 1D

From this daylight nightmare I was awakened, as from many another, by the appearance of my sisters. They came scrambling and calling up the steep rough bank, and parting the long grass found me. Faces of rose, familiar, living; huge shining faces hung up like shields between me and the sky; faces with grins and white teeth (some broken) to be conjured up like genii with a howl, brushing off terror with their broad scoldings and affection. They leaned over me – one, two, three – their mouths smeared with red currants and their hands dripping with juice…

And Marjorie, the eldest, lifted me into her long brown hair, and ran me jogging down the path and through the steep rose-filled garden, and set me down on the cottage doorstep, which was our home, though I couldn't believe it.

14 Now you are going to look at some more letter strings, as you did in Activity 9. You will also look at words which don't follow regular spelling rules.

a Look at the spelling of 'daylight nightmare'. Work with a partner and list other words which are spelt with the letter string *ight*, which has a long 'i' sound when it is said.

b Notice the spelling of 'rough', which is pronounced 'ruff'. The letter string *ough* is not always pronounced as 'uff', however. With your partner, think of examples of words with the letter string *ough* where, although the spelling is the same, the pronunciation is different. Be warned, there are five pronunciations for this letter string!

c Look at the spelling of 'shining', 'dripping' and 'jogging'. Can you and your partner think why the first has a single consonant in the middle (*n*) but the other two have a double (*pp* and *gg*)?

UNIT 1 House and home

Tip

For Activity 14c
Doubling of consonants

The doubling of consonants affects the way words are pronounced as well as their meaning. It makes the vowel which goes before it a 'short' vowel, in other words the vowel is pronounced quickly. (Say the words *pin* and *pine*. Can you hear the difference in the way the letter *i* is pronounced in each one? The *i* in *pin* is a short vowel whereas the *i* in *pine* is a 'long' vowel, with the same sound as the letter I when you recite the alphabet.) Look at and listen to the difference between *dinner* (double *n* with short vowel before it) and *diner* (single *n* with long vowel). This sound rule applies to most words in English, and it is especially useful in helping you to decide whether verbs need a single or a double consonant before the *-ing* and *-ed* ending.

The meaning of some verbs changes according to whether they have one or two consonants after the vowel. For example, how do you spell the *-ing* forms of the verbs *hope* and *hop*? The first is *hoping* (single *p*) and the second is *hopping* (double *p*). They are the same apart from the single or double *p* in the middle, but they mean very different things.

15 You will now be able to plan your own piece of autobiographical writing using all you have learnt in this unit.

   a Look again at the autobiographical texts 1B, 1C and 1D. Work in pairs to collect a list of the things mentioned in them, such as nature, which create the setting for the memory that features in the texts. Think about the setting you will use in your own piece of writing.

   b Which emotions are being described in the three passages? Create a list for each passage. Strong emotions make the best pieces of personal writing because they are dramatic and engaging for the reader.

   c Jot down some ideas for your own first memory. Discuss with your partner which of them would make the best piece of writing, i.e. the one which would convey the strongest emotion.

Cambridge Checkpoint English 7

16 **a** To collect your ideas for your writing, you need to start making some notes on the memory you have chosen to write about. Draw a spider diagram and answer the questions *Who? What? When? Where? Why?*

b An effective piece of autobiographical writing has a setting, characters, actions, feelings and a conclusion, and they are normally in this order. Draw a mind map in your notebook and write in the headings *Setting, Characters, Actions, Feelings, Conclusion*. Make notes for each one.

c Now write about a page as the beginning of your own autobiography.

Key point

Autobiographical writing

- Although autobiographical writing is non-fiction (based on truth), you can make it more interesting for the reader by exaggerating what really happened to make it more dramatic and engaging.
- Strong emotion, and fear in particular, are what makes a memory come alive. It also creates suspense as the reader doesn't know if something frightening will actually happen.
- The weather, season, time of day and details of place create not only the setting but the atmosphere for your memory. Colour is also important for achieving this.
- In first-person narrative your own personality needs to show through in your writing. This can be done by giving the thoughts and feelings you had at the time, as well as your reflections looking back now.
- Try to give the small child's viewpoint to make the experience you are narrating seem real and sympathetic, and perhaps amusing, to the reader. One way of doing this is to make everything seem huge. Another one is to show that children misunderstand situations, which also creates humour.

UNIT 2 Tall tales

There are examples of fantasy fiction in this unit, including tales of horror in prose and verse. You will be able to practise your own narrative writing, including choosing titles, and using direct speech for dramatic effect. You will also look at the use of single dashes and hyphens.

Activities

1. A tale is a short, often anonymous, story which relates imaginary events. Working in pairs, look at the following questions and discuss your ideas in response to them:
   - How many different kinds of tale can you think of?
   - Why do you think people tell each other tales?
   - What do you think makes a good tale? Give some examples.

Text 2A

Jim, the boy who ran away

There was a Boy whose name was Jim;
His Friends were very good to him.
They gave him Tea, and Cakes, and Jam,
And slices of delicious Ham,
And Chocolate with pink inside
And little Tricycles to ride,
And read him stories through and through,
And even took him to the Zoo —
But there it was the <u>dreadful</u> Fate
Befell him, which I now **relate**.

You know — or at least you *ought* to know,
For I have often told you so —
That Children never are allowed
To leave their Nurses in a Crowd;
Now this was Jim's especial **Foible**,
He ran away when he was able,
And on this <u>inauspicious</u> day
He slipped his hand and ran away!
He hadn't gone a yard when — Bang!
With open Jaws, a Lion sprang,
And hungrily began to eat
The Boy: beginning at his feet.

Now, just imagine how it feels
When first your toes and then your heels,
And then, by **gradual** degrees,
Your shins and ankles, calves and knees,
Are slowly eaten, bit by bit.
No wonder Jim <u>detested</u> it!
No wonder that he shouted 'Hi!'
The Honest Keeper heard his cry;
Though very fat, he almost ran
To help the little gentleman.
'Ponto!' he ordered as he came
(For Ponto was the Lion's name),
'Ponto!' he cried, with angry Frown,
'Let go, Sir! Down, Sir! Put it down!'
The Lion made a sudden Stop,
He let the Dainty **Morsel** drop,
And slunk **reluctant** to his Cage,
Snarling with Disappointed <u>Rage</u>.
But when he bent down over Jim,
The Honest Keeper's Eyes were dim.
The Lion having reached his Head . . .
The miserable Boy was dead!
When Nurse informed his Parents, they
Were more Concerned than I can say:
His Mother, as She dried her eyes,
Said, 'Well – it gives me no surprise,
He would not do as he was told!'
His Father, who was self-controlled,
Bade all the children round attend
To James' miserable end,
And always keep a-hold of Nurse
For fear of finding something worse.

Hilaire Belloc

2
- **a** The poem in Text 2A is a cautionary tale. What do you think this means?
- **b** Illustrate the text with a simple drawing to show what happens to Jim in the tale.
- **c** Discuss in pairs whether you like the tale or not, giving your reasons. Think about the humour, the description and the rhyme.

UNIT 2 Tall tales

3 In this activity you will be looking at the vocabulary in the poem in Text 2A. You may need to use a dictionary or thesaurus to help you, but first try to work out the meaning of the words from their context, i.e. from the meaning of the other words around them.

   a Find the five words in bold in Text 2A. Decide on the part of speech of each of the words. Give synonyms (words with a similar meaning) for the words as they are used in the poem, using the same part of speech.

   b Find the words in Text 2A which are not at the beginning of a line but which start with a capital letter. What part of speech are they?

   c Now find the underlined words in Text 2A. Match them with their correct meanings in each line:

dreadful	fatal	terrible	predicted
befell	fell on	struck	happened to
inauspicious	unlucky	unhappy	unimportant
detested	examined	hated	ignored
rage	annoyance	sadness	fury

4 What do you think is the moral, or message, of the cautionary tale in Text 2A? Think about what happens in the poem and the characters in it. What do you notice about how the poem is arranged (its form)? Copy the table below into your notebook and complete it with your ideas.

Moral / Message	Content / Events	Characters	Form / Layout

5 a In his cautionary tale about Jim, Hilaire Belloc has used direct speech. In other words, he has given the actual words spoken by the characters. Look at how direct speech is used in Text 2A. What do you think is the effect of using direct speech in tales?

   b Work with a partner and list all the verbs you can think of which can be used to follow direct speech (you can find some of these verbs in Text 2A, for example). Compare lists with the rest of the class. Which pair has thought of the most?

   c Why do you think it is better to use a range of verbs with direct speech than to always use *said*?

6 **a** As a class, collect a list of warnings which parents might wish to convey to children. For example, children should not eat too many sweets.

  b Working in pairs, choose one you like and discuss some story ideas for your own cautionary tale.

  c Agree on a suitable name for your child character (and think about what will rhyme with it). Agree on a title for the tale. Give it the same form as the title in Text 2A: 'Name, the boy/girl who …'

7 **a** Plan your story in a series of five boxes like a comic strip. Give speech bubbles to the characters in each box so that they can explain what is happening.

  b Decide which bits of dramatic speech to include in your tale, and decide how to express the moral at the end of the tale to make the warning to children clear.

  c Read the key point below about language features, then write your own cautionary tale. The first line should be similar to that in Text 2A: 'There was a … whose name was …' (Your cautionary tale can be shorter than the one in Text 2A.)

Key point

Language features of cautionary tales

- In Text 2A each pair of lines is rhymed (the words at the end of the lines contain the same or a similar vowel sound).
- The number of sounds (syllables or beats) in each line is eight, arranged as four pairs. Read one of the lines in the poem and count the beats on your fingers as you read. The second beat in each pair is stressed, so it has the rhythm dee-<u>dum</u>, dee-<u>dum</u>, dee-<u>dum</u>, dee-<u>dum</u>. (This poetic metre, or pattern, is called iambic tetrameter.) See if you can copy this pattern in your own cautionary tale.
- You find quite a lot of exclamations and questions in a cautionary tale, especially in dialogue, because these add drama and strong feeling or humour.
- Humorous names, like Ponto, are used for comic effect. Try to use some in your tale.

UNIT 2 Tall tales

Text 2B is an example of an urban legend, a short, popular, modern tale spread orally or in writing, and told as if it is true.

Text 2B

One cold winter night, sixteen-year-old Kathy was home alone. Her parents had gone out to a dinner party. It had been snowing all that afternoon, but had recently stopped. After studying for a few hours Kathy decided to relax by lying on the couch and watching TV in the living room. The television was in front of the glass door that led to the back garden.

By midnight Kathy's parents still hadn't come home and she was terrified because she thought she had caught a glimpse of a very strange-looking man staring at her, standing outside the glass sliding door behind the television. Shaking with fear, she pulled a blanket over her head and grabbed the phone by her side. She called the police and in a few minutes officers arrived.

Kathy told them about the strange man who had been standing outside, staring in through the glass.

The police opened the sliding door and looked around. They explained that there could not have been anyone standing outside as there would be footprints in the snow. They told her that she was probably just overtired and had imagined it. As the officers were about to leave, one of them stopped behind the couch Kathy was sitting on. His jaw dropped as he shouted, 'Look here!' Kathy looked: there were wet footprints on the carpet behind the couch. She hadn't seen the man outside the door; she'd seen his reflection when he was standing behind her in the room!

Text 2C is another example of an urban legend.

Text 2C

About a month ago in Soweto, a man was on the side of the road hitch-hiking on a very dark night and in the middle of a storm.

No car went by, and the rain was so heavy he could hardly see a few metres ahead of him. Suddenly, a car came towards him and stopped. Without thinking about it, the man got in and closed the door, realising too late that there was nobody in the driver's seat. The car started slowly. The man looked at the road, and he saw that a bend was approaching.

He was terrified, but just before he hit the curve a hand appeared through the window and moved the steering wheel. This happened again and again; every time there was a bend in the road, the hand took control. The man escaped from the car and ran to the nearest township.

Wet and in shock, he went into a café and told everybody there about the petrifying experience he had been through, and they were stunned into silence.

About half an hour later, two men entered the café and one said to the other, 'Look, Lewa, there's that idiot who got into our car when we were pushing it.'

8   Read Texts 2B and 2C.

   a How would you define the content of an urban legend?

   b Why do you think this type of tale exists?

   c Decide which of the urban legends in Texts 2B and 2C is in your opinion more scary. Explain your reasons to the class.

   d Share with the class any other urban legends you have heard.

   e Work in pairs to make a list of the features which make urban legends scary.

9 a Decide on an idea for your own urban legend. If you can't think of a new idea, you can adapt one you have already heard or use the plot-line of a scary film or book. Use the tip about urban legends to help you.

   b Draft your story of about half a page. Use your answers to Activity 8 and the ideas in the key point on the next page about writing a short story to help you.

   c Practise reading your story, and then read it out to the class. As you read, use changes of speed, pauses and expression in your voice to make it seem more frightening.

For Activity 9a
Urban legends

There will usually be crime or violence, or at least the threat of it, in an urban legend. The victim is always someone alone and vulnerable. Don't overstate anything gruesome, but concentrate on how close the victim came to having a terrible experience. Bear in mind that the victim is usually someone naïve, who does not realise the danger they are in or that they are being tricked. At the same time, they are ordinary people and we sympathise with them because we see the situation through their eyes and it could happen to any of us.

UNIT 2 Tall tales

Key point

Writing a short story

- The endings to all short narratives are more effective if they are unpredictable, to keep up the suspense and provide a memorable and often ironic (something unexpected, undesired or undeserved) twist.
- It is important to know before you begin your story how it is going to end, so that you can plant the clues along the way, but without revealing too much.
- To keep up the narrative pace, it is important not to waste any words. It is the events which matter, not descriptions or details. On the other hand, it is important to build up suspense by not reaching the conclusion too soon.
- Direct speech is often a good way of creating fear or urgency, but it should be kept for the dramatic or comic moments, and not used for ordinary conversation between characters.

Text 2D

Mini-sagas

A saga is a long prose tale of the adventures and achievements of a hero. A mini-saga is a narrative of exactly 50 words. Mini-sagas are often a mixture of sad and amusing ideas, and have surprise twists at the end.

These five mini-sagas were written by Secondary 1 students.

1
I had longed to get rid of him for weeks. Finally, I had the chance. I climbed the stairs, cautiously entered the room – and saw him grinning in the mirror. The door slammed. A cry of agony, and it was over. Wreathed in blood, my tooth dangled on the string.

2
I am thrown in with a crowd. The door slams shut. I hear gushing water. I feel redness oozing from me, colouring the water. Gasping for air, I am knocked out by arms and legs. I come round hanging on the washing line – a red sock among pale pink laundry.

3
Another dawn. The frosty walk to the front line, heart pounding, chest tight. He stands exposed,

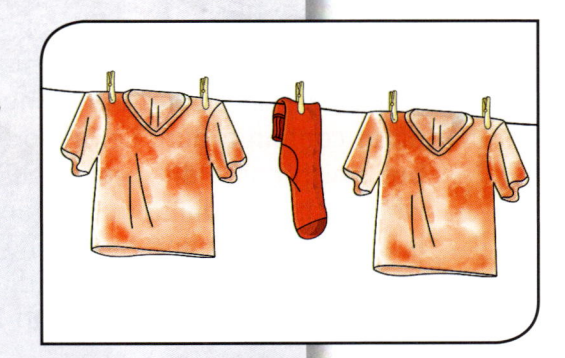

awaiting the inevitable onslaught. The first missiles whistle overhead. The enemy's roar rises to a crescendo. He must counter-attack, already knowing the futility and tasting defeat. 'Alright, 3C, settle down. Let's have some quiet!'

4
My teacher, Mrs Bailey, wears a pair of steel-rimmed spectacles. They're rounded, and perched there, glaring at you. One day they fell! She perched them on again. The left lens said, 'I hate looking at books. I want holidays in the sun.' Mrs Bailey only sees half the class now.

5
Sitting, watching, goggling at the box, his legs begin to shrink. His bottom grows fatter and fatter, filling the armchair he sits in, slowly at first, then faster and faster. His eyes grow square instead of round. His head slowly turns to jelly – from sitting in front of the telly.

10 a Read the five mini-sagas in Text 2D. Which of them have unexpected endings? How have these been created?

  b Look at the five mini-sagas again. Make a list of the narrators and subjects of each of them. Which of them are unusual, and what is the effect?

  c Mini-sagas normally have a title but the titles in Text 2D have been removed. In small groups, discuss possible titles for the five mini-sagas and decide on a good title for each one. Look at the key point to help you.

Key point

Short story titles

Short story titles usually consist of between one and three words. The best ones sound intriguing but do not give away the story. They often contain a pun, i.e. a word which sounds like another word but which has a different spelling and meaning, or the same word which has two different meanings. You can give a hint that there is a double meaning by adding a question mark at the end. You could also use the pattern 'adjective + noun' as your title. This is a common form of title for short stories as well as poems and novels.

UNIT 2 Tall tales

11 **a** Mini-saga 3 relies on an extended image. When we first read it, we think we are reading about a soldier preparing for battle, but in the last sentence the real situation (a teacher preparing to face his class) becomes clear. List the words which give the idea of a battle.

b Sometimes the meaning of a mini-saga is left for you to work out. What do you think mini-saga 4 is saying about Mrs Bailey?

c If mini-saga 5 were a poem, where do you think would be the best place to start new lines? Discuss how giving it a different form (or layout) changes the effect of the story.

12 Punctuation and grammar are very important in very short narratives, for saving words and for creating tone (emotion). In the five mini-sagas in Text 2D, find examples of the following and think about how they are used. Discuss in pairs what effect is created.
- present participles (*-ing* words) in mini-sagas 2, 3, 4 and 5
- dashes in mini-sagas 1, 2 and 5
- direct speech in mini-sagas 3 and 4

13 **a** Draft two different mini-sagas, trying out the ideas you have discussed in your previous answers. Look at the advice in the key point box about writing a mini-saga to help you too.

b Reduce each of your drafts to exactly 50 words without losing any of the meaning. This can be done by:
- removing unnecessary words, not needed by the grammar or the meaning
- using compound adjectives (two words joined by a hyphen, e.g. *steel-rimmed*)
- replacing phrasal with single verbs (e.g. *to be afraid of* → *to fear*)
- using full stops rather than simple sentence connectives (*and, but, so*)
- using dashes, which also create dramatic effect
- using direct speech concisely
- giving it a title which gives a clue to the meaning.

c Swap your mini-sagas with a partner. Decide which of your partner's mini-sagas is better and should be read out to the class.

Key point

Writing a mini-saga

- Mini-sagas are in every sense a miniature narrative, i.e. they usually contain at least one character, an event, the passage of time, and possibly some speech.
- The narrator may be unusual, or the event may be seen from an unusual perspective, like an object photographed from a strange angle which is then not immediately recognisable.
- Their aim is to make the reader amused or sympathetic towards the character.
- They need a strong ending to be effective, so make the last word(s) significant.
- The title, if carefully chosen, can be part of the story; it should say something important, or create a mystery, in a very concise way.
- There isn't space for many adjectives or adverbs, but with the right choice of verb you shouldn't need them; make the verbs do the work in telling the story. Present participles save words.
- Every word should carry weight, and it is even better if one word can be made to do the work of two, as in a pun.
- The very best mini-sagas have a rhythm too, a satisfactory sound and a shape to the sentences, as in mini-saga 5.

Text 2E

This is an extract from *The Hound of the Baskervilles* by Arthur Conan Doyle.

A terrible scream – a prolonged yell of horror and anguish – burst out of the silence of the moor. That frightful cry turned the blood to ice in my veins. I gasped. 'What is it? What does it mean?'

Holmes had sprung to his feet, and I saw his dark, athletic outline at the door of the hut, his shoulders stooping, his head thrust forward, his face peering into the darkness.

'Hush!' he whispered. 'Hush!'

The cry had been loud on account of its vehemence, but it had pealed out from somewhere far off on the shadowy plain. Now it burst upon our ears, nearer, louder, more urgent than before.

'Where is it?' Holmes whispered; and I knew from the thrill of his voice that he, the man of iron, was shaken to the soul.

'There, I think.' I pointed into the darkness.

Again the agonised cry swept through the silent night, louder and much nearer than ever. And a new sound mingled with it, a deep, muttered rumble, musical and yet menacing, rising and falling like the low, constant murmur of the sea.

'The hound!' cried Holmes. 'Come, Watson, come! Great heavens, if we are too late!'

He had started running swiftly over the moor, and I had followed at his heels. But now from somewhere among the broken ground immediately in front of us there came one last despairing yell, and then a dull, heavy thud. We halted and listened. Not another sound broke the heavy silence of the windless night.

I saw Holmes put his hand to his forehead like a man distracted. He stamped his feet upon the ground.

'He has beaten us, Watson. We are too late.'

'No, no, surely not!'

Blindly we ran through the gloom, blundering against boulders, forcing our way through gorse bushes, panting up hills and rushing down slopes, heading always in the direction whence those dreadful sounds had come. At every rise Holmes looked eagerly round him, but the shadows were thick upon the moor, and nothing moved upon its dreary face.

'Hark, what is that?'

A low moan had fallen upon our ears. There it was again upon our left! On that side a ridge of rocks ended in a sheer cliff which overlooked a stone-strewn slope. On its jagged face was spread-eagled some dark, irregular object. As we ran towards it the vague outline hardened into a definite shape. It was a prostrate man face downward upon the ground, the head doubled under him at a horrible angle, the shoulders rounded and the body hunched together as if in the act of throwing a somersault. So grotesque was the attitude that I could not for the instant realise that that moan had been the passing of his soul. Not a whisper, not a rustle, rose now from the dark figure over which we stooped. Holmes laid his hand upon him and held it up again with an exclamation of horror.

14 **a** Text 2E is an extract from a Sherlock Holmes story about a giant supernatural Hound of the Baskervilles. Read it aloud with different voices for the narrator and the direct speech of Holmes and his fellow detective, Watson. How does the use of dialogue add to the effect of the passage?

b Look again at the examples of direct speech in Text 2E. What can you say about:
  i the length and amount of direct speech?
  ii its content?
  iii its punctuation?

c Text 2E contains many examples of the typical features of horror texts. These are used to create suspense (making the reader wait and become tense) in the story. Copy the table below into your notebook and complete it with descriptions and examples of the different features.

Feature	Description	Example / Quotation
Time of day		
Setting		
Type of characters		
Speed of action		
Sentence length		
Use of repetition		
Sense of sound		
Sense of sight		
Vocabulary		
Imagery		

15 Referring to the table in Activity 14, plan and write a page of suspense/horror that makes use of as many of the features of Text 2E as possible. You could use the same two characters, Holmes and Watson, in a different situation, or you could make up your own characters. Include some dialogue for dramatic effect.

UNIT 3 Favourite things

This unit is about the things you like to do, see, have and eat, and it contains passages and poems about colours and seasons. The skills you will practise are making notes, building sentences, using present participles, the use of 'would', putting ideas in order, and using adjectives and images effectively. You will also learn more about form, rhyme and metre in poetry.

Activities

1 When you make notes of what someone is saying or has written, you record only the key phrases as a kind of summary.

   a Work in pairs and ask your partner to tell you the things they like doing, and make notes.

   b Ask your partner what they like to eat, and make notes.

   c Using your notes, tell the rest of the class what you have discovered about your partner's favourite pastimes and food, in that order.

Key point

Making notes

Making notes is a way of collecting relevant information for a task based on a reading or listening passage, and it's a very important skill for summary writing. You need to ignore all the examples and minor details and just get down the essential facts or ideas. There is no need to write down whole sentences – just the key phrases. You can group them, expand them or join them together later, if necessary, or use them as the basis for revision or for planning a speaking or writing task.

2 **a** Spend a few minutes making a list of your favourite possessions. Then consider which ones are really the most important to you, and reduce it to three items.

   b Now choose the most precious item and write down some adjectives, including size, shape and colour, to describe it.

   c Add an explanation of why this object is your most prized possession, then use your description to tell the class about it.

My favourite things

Raindrops on roses and whiskers on kittens,
Bright copper kettles and warm woollen mittens,
Brown paper packages tied up with strings,
These are a few of my favourite things.

Cream coloured ponies and crisp apple strudels,
Door bells and sleigh bells and schnitzel with noodles.
Wild geese that fly with the moon on their wings,
These are a few of my favourite things.

Girls in white dresses with blue satin sashes,
Snowflakes that stay on my nose and eyelashes,
Silver white winters that melt into springs,
These are a few of my favourite things.

When the dog bites, when the bee stings,
When I'm feeling sad,
I simply remember my favourite things,
And then I don't feel so bad.

Rodgers and Hammerstein

3 Look at the following phrases from the song:
- bright copper kettles
- warm woollen mittens
- brown paper packages
- blue satin sashes.

Work in pairs and try to work out what the rule is for ordering more than one adjective before a noun. Then put these strings of adjectives in the right order before the noun that is given. You should be able to tell which order sounds better.
- wooden, painted, ancient + statue
- gold, valuable, old + ring
- African, green, miniature + parrot

UNIT **3** Favourite things

Key point

Adjectival order

When you are using more than one adjective in front of a noun, there is a general rule for the order they should go in, which is: opinion, size, shape, age, colour, nationality, substance – for example, 'the beautiful, large, rectangular, ancient, pink, Indian, silk rug'. Usually, however, we do not use more than three adjectives in a row before a noun, so the main thing to remember is that size, shape and age go before colour, and that colour goes before where the thing comes from and what it is made of. That's why in the song 'copper', 'woollen', 'paper' and 'satin' are all placed next to the noun. Remember to put a comma between items in a list, i.e. between each of the adjectives, but not between the last one and the noun.

4
a As you read or listen to the words of the song in Text 3A, count the number of syllables in the lines, and on a copy of the text underline the ones which you think are stressed, or emphasised.

b Look at the last words in each line. Can you say what the rhyme pattern is in the verses and the final chorus?

c On your copy of the song, find and circle examples of alliteration (words close together which begin with the same sound, e.g. *few, favourite*) and assonance (words close together which contain the same vowel sound, e.g. *whiskers, kittens*).

d Now that you have looked at some poetic features, think of your own extra verse to add to the song before the chorus. Make sure that it fits the rhyme scheme and metre (number of syllables per line and how they are stressed) and try to use some alliteration and assonance.

e Read – or sing! – your new verse to the class.

The theme of the next part of the unit, containing Texts 3B–3D, is food.

Text 3B

I love pasta!

Pasta! My favourite food has to be pasta. It's only flour and water, but it makes delicious meals. It was being eaten in Italy a thousand years ago – and the Italians know about good food. It's also the land of pizza, my second favourite!

If you make it yourself, instead of buying it in packets in the supermarket, it tastes wonderful, but it's hard work because there are many stages: it has to be kneaded, rolled, cut and dried. This was made easier by the invention of machines to do this work in the early 19th century. Pasta's taste buddy is the tomato, of course. You can't imagine pasta without tomatoes can you? It would be like bread without butter. But for the Italians pasta is just the starter, the first of three courses for every meal, and they often eat it with just olive oil and herbs.

What I love about pasta is that it comes in all shapes and sizes, and you can choose which one suits your mood, and the sauce accompaniment. Some of them have a stuffing, some of them are difficult to twirl on your fork, and there are different colours too: white, green and orange, depending on whether egg, spinach or tomato has been added to the durum wheat paste.

So every pasta meal can be as different and as challenging as you want it to be. There are several hundred varieties, coming from all the different regions of Italy, and there's a reason why every one of them looks the way it does, and has the name it does: little worms, little ears, little tongues, butterflies, shells. Such interesting and appropriate names! Apparently long stringy types are best for smooth sauces, while grooves and shapes hold chunkier ones. My favourite has to be slippery, slurpy, snaky spaghetti!

5
a Skim read Text 3B, then scan read it again (see the key point on page 9 about skimming and scanning). Make notes of the facts about pasta.

b Turn your notes into five sentences, and then link those which belong together because they express similar ideas. Think of different ways you can join them, using *and*, *but*, *so* and *or*, as well as present participles (*-ing* words).

c Now try to turn your five sentences into just three sentences by doing some more joining. Then work in pairs and compare your summary of Text 3B with your partner's.

UNIT 3 Favourite things

6 After reading Text 3B, you're feeling hungry and you decide to cook some pasta for yourself. You've found a recipe, Text 3C, on a cooking website, but you notice that it won't work.

Text 3C

Pasta recipe

- Boil the water in the pan.
- Drain away the water using a colander.
- Put the pasta into the boiling water, about 75 g per person.
- Fill a large saucepan with water.
- Serve the pasta onto plates.
- Pour a pre-warmed sauce over the plates of pasta.
- Test that the pasta is cooked by tasting a piece on a fork.
- Stir the pasta so that it is separate and doesn't stick together.
- Add some salt to the water before it boils.
- Check on the packet how long the pasta needs to cook.

a The ten stages of the recipe in Text 3C are in the wrong order. Discuss in pairs how to sequence the instructions so that the recipe can be followed properly.

b Think of your own favourite meal and list the stages required to make it. You don't have to be exact about the ingredients or cooking times, just know which order to do things in.

c Write out your recipe, using the same kind of language as in Text 3C. Start each sentence with an imperative (command) verb and keep the sentences short and simple. Swap your recipe with a partner, who will tell you whether you've missed anything out and whether it makes sense to do things in that order.

Menu

Pad Thai
A delicious, delicate Thai dish of succulent stir-fried rice noodles, blended with egg, tender bean sprouts, rosy shrimp, roast peanuts, and spicy seasonings.

Fish Sayadeyah
A mouth-watering dish prepared with chunks of fresh fish garnished with whole fried almonds, crunchy pine nuts and sliced, crispy, fried onions, accompanied by rice simmered in a rich fish broth with tasty spices that give the rice a warm, deep brown colour.

Tagine
The rich and aromatic casseroles that form the basis of traditional Moroccan cooking: sumptuous lamb tagine in a medley of exotic dates, tasty apricots, and pistachios, or tangy chicken tagine with preserved lemon, green olives and aromatic thyme.

UNIT 3 Favourite things

7 **a** Menus use a particular kind of vocabulary. What do you notice about the language in the menu items in Text 3D? Why do you think this type of vocabulary is used?

b The grammar in menus is also distinctive. What do you notice about the sentences in the menu? Why do you think this kind of grammar is used?

c Using the same style, describe your own favourite meal. Use lots of adjectives, including colours and taste words, to make it sound very appealing to the appetite.

8 In the previous activity you looked at descriptive language to describe your favourite meal. Of course, there are other favourite things which you can describe too.

a Take part in a class vote on the following things, and make a note of the results for each one:
  i favourite colour
  ii favourite time of day
  iii favourite season or festival.

b Why do you think the winners got the most votes? Discuss reasons for the choices of the favourites.

c Words, and especially adjectives, have positive and negative connotations (ideas or feelings suggested by a word). The word *bright*, for example, is usually positive whereas *old* is usually negative. Copy the table below and complete it by giving a plus or minus value to the colours, using a scale of +5 to –5, and saying which things are associated with them.

Colour	Value	Associations
brown		
purple		
pink		
orange		
grey		
white		

Cambridge Checkpoint English 7

The next part of the unit is on the theme of favourite colours. Text 3E has American spelling.

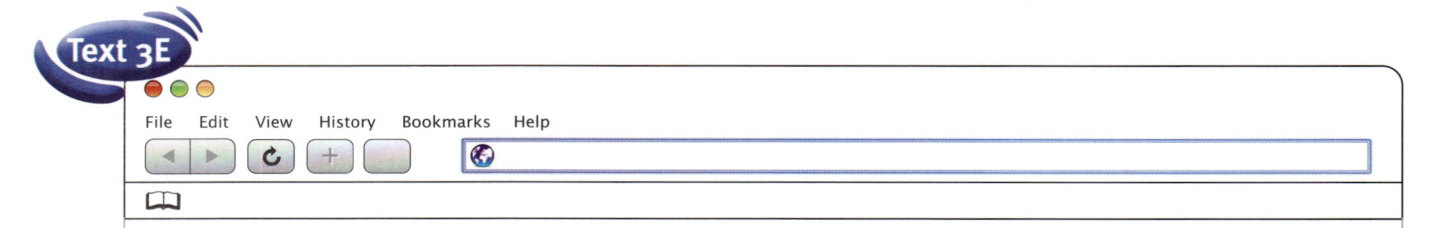

Text 3E

The United Colors of Benetton

'All the colors of the world' was one of the first slogans to appear in Benetton ads, and was later altered to 'United Colors of Benetton'. The concept of united colors was such a strong one that for the first time in its history, the company adopted the slogan as its actual logo. For the first time in the history of commercial trademarks, the slogan United Colors of Benetton became a trademark, a trademark that became the driving force behind the 'United Colors' message, which formed the basis of the advertising visuals designed to create a growing network of 'United People'. These images showed youth of both sexes and every skin tone, who conveyed a message of harmony, energy and joy.

9 a Write an explanation of how the colours used in the photograph make the products seem more desirable.

  b Many people's favourite colour is one of the main colours (red, yellow, green and blue). Write an explanation of why you think these colours have such a powerful effect.

UNIT 3 Favourite things

c Write an explanation of the double meaning of the slogan 'The United Colors of Benetton'.

10 Specific colours conjure up ideas in the reader's mind. For example, navy is a more definite shade than just 'dark blue', and it has connotations of the sea and ships.

  a Which words come to your mind when you think of the following colours?

  gold   silver   beige   ginger   turquoise

  b Look up the exact shade conveyed by the following colour words and use them appropriately in a sentence for each.

  violet   azure   charcoal   amber   olive

  c Compound colour adjectives can be even more specific, for example *mint-green*. Work in pairs and see how many compound adjectives you can think of.

Text 3F

Grey

Grey is the light at the end of the day.
Grey is the ancient head full of wisdom.
Grey is the perilous path leading to the cave.
Grey is the silken spider's web in the corner.
Grey is the smoke from the factory chimney.

Grey are the waves of the angry sea.
Grey are the stones of the prison wall.
Grey are the clouds gathering on the horizon.
Grey are the birds that fly away from the cold.
Grey are the eyes that are glued to TV.

11 a Read the poem in Text 3F around the class. Look at the metaphors in the poem. What emotions and experiences does it suggest that the colour grey is associated with?

  b Can you think of other images which could have been used for the colour grey? Work in pairs to create a list. Are they similar to or different from the ideas expressed in Text 3F?

  c Make a list of all the different shades of red you can think of (you may need a thesaurus to help you) and then create images for those red colours, for example, comparing scarlet to a poppy.

d Using your image list, write a poem called 'Red' in the same form and length as the poem 3F, each line beginning with a different shade of red.

e Read out your poem. The class can vote on which is the best 'Red' poem and say why it is the best. You could also illustrate and display your poems.

The theme of the next part of the unit is favourite seasons and times of the day and year.

Text 3G

This is a letter from a Chinese student to his penfriend, describing his favourite day of the year.

Dear Noor,

I am very excited that tomorrow is our biggest event of the year, when we celebrate New Year, the first day of the lunar calendar. This has its origin in folklore, and celebrates the time when people try to scare away a demon called 'Festival' by using the colour red and setting off firecrackers. Red symbolises luck, peace and fortune. The fireworks also bring in new hope for the future and get rid of the bad luck from the past year. There is a twelve-year cycle of animal names; this is the year of the Rabbit and next year will be the Dragon, a really special one.

Tonight we shall watch a spring gala of comedies and songs performed in traditional costume, lasting for four or five hours. We shall eat dumplings for dinner, which occurs exactly at midnight. Our house and the street outside have been decorated with red silk banners and messages of good will.

Tomorrow we shall give presents to family members and friends to wish them well in the coming year. We must say 'Xin Nian Kuai Le' to everyone we meet, which means 'Happy New Year'. Gifts of money are given to children. In the evening we shall watch the TV programme which everyone watches on this day. It is the most exciting day of the year for Chinese people. Wishing you 'Xin Nian Kuai Le'.

Your pen pal,
Hongwei

UNIT 3 Favourite things

12 **a** Does your country have a national costume or traditional dress? In groups, discuss what it consists of and what it represents. This may involve some research. Draw and label the costumes for males and females.

b In your group, decide which colours are most closely associated with your culture (e.g. red and yellow are the favourite colours of the Chinese), and discuss what they represent. Think about:
  i your national flag colours
  ii your school uniform colours
  iii your national football team colours.

c Imagine that you are Hongwei's penfriend. Write a letter back to him describing your favourite feast day of the year.

Text 3H

This is a poem by a child about her favourite season.

Autumn for me is

an indescribable earthy smell,
skies palest blue to crimson hue,
mists unravelled by the sun,
spiders' webs sparkling with dew,
a lonely owl hooting in the night,
smoke from bonfires heavenward trailing,
birds' nests looking frayed . . . forgotten,
rose-red apples, ripe and sweet,
wind-whirling, swirling, twirling leaves
bracken-brown undergrowth, heather-covered hills
last petals falling to the ground
last seeds floating – whither bound?
a mellow season
    in between
a golden gleam
    – that's autumn.

Helen Mackay

13 a You will have noticed that the poem in Text 3H is full of colours. List all those you can find in the poem.

  b What can you say about the form/layout of the poem in Text 3H? Are there any special or unusual features you have noticed?

  c Sound is important in the poem in Text 3H. What can you say about how it has been used?

Text 3I

This is a poem about another child's favourite time of day.

Evening

When silver moonbeams fill the sky,
That is the time that I love best,
To hear the blackbird's <u>startled</u> cry,
As she flies homeward to her nest.
I hear the nightingale <u>sweetly</u> singing,
As daisies droop their weary head;
It sounds like little church bells ringing,
While the sunset <u>glows</u> a fiery red.
A <u>whispering</u> breeze sweeps through the boughs
Of old oak trees which stand so still;
Herdsmen are driving home the cows,
As the sun sinks slowly behind the hill.
The evening is a <u>lovely</u> sight,
As stars begin to light the sky;
The owl waits for the coming night,
To hunt for prey she then must fly.
When silver moonbeams fill the sky
The harvest mice go scampering by.

14 a Work in pairs and together agree on the definition of the rhyme scheme and metre of the poem in Text 3I.

  b If you were asked to divide the poem into separate verses, how many would you create, and where would you make the divisions, and why?

  c Replace the five underlined words in the poem with other words which would fit the meaning and the metre. Comment on why you think they would or wouldn't be good replacements.

UNIT 3 Favourite things

15 **a** Decide on your favourite month, season or time of day, and collect ideas and images which you associate with it. Arrange your ideas in a spider diagram.

  b Draft a poem using your collection of descriptive words and images. Try to use some of the ideas for content and form which you have talked about and collected during this unit, such as the use of specific colours. Think about whether you want to divide it into verses. You can use rhyme if you wish, but you don't have to.

  c Ask your partner to read your poem and suggest improvements to content and form.

Key point

Using rhyme in poetry

Rhyme makes poems easier to remember, and sometimes adds humour to comic verse. Generally speaking, the older the poem is, the more likely it is to have a regular pattern of rhyming. Poems do not have to rhyme, however, and it is better not to use words in a poem just because they provide a rhyme, especially if this reduces the quality of the meaning or makes it sound silly. Rhyme should sound natural, as though it's the perfect word to use.

Text 3J

My perfect day

I'd get up between six and seven, which is when I wake up. I'd go downstairs before anyone else in the family was up to feed my outdoor pets and take my dog for a walk. I live in the country so there are quiet places to go where no one else goes.

I'd return for breakfast, by which time the rest of the family would be up. I'd have pancakes with golden syrup, because they're a treat which we don't have on normal school days. Then my friends would come to my house and we'd play games in the garden, if the weather was good, or in my bedroom. We'd lose track of the time and no one would come and see what we were doing or tell us off for making a mess. I wouldn't have any homework to do, of course, or any chores like tidying my room, so I wouldn't have to do anything I didn't want to do.

There'd be a big lunch, with all my favourite food, including chocolate cake, and afterwards we'd watch a DVD, something just out and that I'd been looking forward to seeing. It would probably be a comedy or a fantasy film. We'd lie on the floor with cushions and have some popcorn or other snacks while we watched. After that we'd go out to get some exercise, either for a bike ride or to play sport. We have a basketball court nearby and that's my favourite game at the moment.

Before the evening meal – which would be pizza or fried chicken – I'd go for a walk with my best friend and my dog, down to the nearby river, and we'd just talk about everything happening at school, and to the people we know, and about our next holidays. I'd probably take some photos with my phone or digital camera for a laugh. If it were really hot we'd swim and then dry off lying on the river bank, with a cool drink. I'd take my MP3 player and we'd listen to some of my favourite bands, sharing the ear piece between us.

At the end of the day, after my friend had left, I'd join my family for supper and find out what they'd been doing all day. I'd play a board game with my brother or sister, if I could persuade them. We'd sit outside on the balcony and watch the sunset and listen to the bird and animal noises if it was summer, or in winter we'd sit on the rug in front of the fire. About nine o'clock I'd go to my room, feeling pleasantly tired and ready to read an exciting adventure story in bed until I fell asleep.

16 a On a copy of the text, underline the first word in each sentence of Text 3J, and notice that they are mostly different to avoid the repetition of *Then* or *I*.

  b Now find and underline all the instances of the verb *would* (often contracted to 'd'), which is being used to form conditional sentences. In other words, the passage is not describing what happened or will happen, only something the speaker would like to happen.

  c What is your opinion of this account of a perfect day? Does it sound perfect to you? Think of reasons why or why not.

UNIT 3 Favourite things

17 **a** Make notes in a mind map for your own piece of personal reflective writing called 'My perfect day'. Use the tip below to help you.

b Write a draft of about one page. Remember to write it in the conditional tense, using 'I would . . .'

c Edit your draft, looking for ways to remove repetition of vocabulary and vary your sentence structure, and, of course, correct any errors. Write a final version to give in.

> **Tip**
>
> **For Activity 17a**
> **'My perfect day' reflective writing**
>
> When writing chronologically (i.e. in the order in which things happen), use time references such as mealtimes and bedtime to give the piece structure. You can borrow ideas from Text 3J, but make them your own by changing the details about what you would do and what you would eat. The more detail you use, the more original and interesting your writing will be. For instance, the passage could have used some names, and it could have given details of the kind of outdoor pets and the board game. The reader can't become engaged in your writing if he or she can't picture what you are talking about. Don't forget about paragraphs, which show a change of time, place, action or topic. Notice that in Text 3J there is a change of paragraph for each part of the day.

UNIT 4 School stories

This unit focuses on school life and stories set in school. You will learn about creating character and setting, and you will practise predicting and planning, using imagery and detail, as well as dialogue and reported speech, to make your writing more varied and engaging.

Activities

1 Much of your time is spent at school, so this is an important part of your life and one which provides you with many experiences which you can make use of in your creative writing.

a In pairs, interview each other about your school life so far. Ask each other the following questions and make notes on what your partner says (see the key point on making notes on page 25).
- How many schools have you attended? Where were they?
- What type of school were they?
- How were they different from each other?
- Which school or class did you enjoy most?
- Which teachers have you admired most?
- What are your favourite subjects?

b Arrange the notes from your interview into about half a page of writing.

c Read what you have written to the class to tell them about your partner's school experiences.

Key point

Expanding notes

When you turn a list of notes into a piece of continuous writing – as you need to do when turning a plan into an exam answer – first put the notes into a logical order so that one idea leads into the next, and ideas which are related are expressed in the same sentence or in linked sentences. The writing must be in full sentences and should no

UNIT 4 School stories

longer sound like a list. You need to produce an answer which is long enough to fulfil the task but which does not go over the length limit you have been set.

Text 4A

In this extract from *The Endless Steppe* by Esther Hautzig, the young Esther goes to a new school in Russia when her family is exiled from Poland in 1941.

The morning I was to go to school for the first time, I woke up in a blackness as mysterious as the heart of a dark forest, the sounds nearby its strange beat. But the howl of a wolf way out in the country gave me my bearings.

I took up my little notebook, and a small stub of pencil, my only academic possessions. How long would they last? How small could I write?

I quickly got dressed, as warmly as I could, although deep winter had not yet arrived. On went my one and only coat. I was ready to go. It never occurred to me that for a child to walk alone down a deserted Siberian road, so obviously a stranger, required some courage. I was too busy trying to rehearse the Russian alphabet I would need to know in my new school.

In room number five, a few children in caps and coats were seated at their desks watching the teacher write on the blackboard. She turned when I came in and looked at me so **severely** my heart sank.

'You must be Esther Rudomin. From Poland. Your Russian will be poor.' It was as if she was reading from a dossier that would determine some sort of punishment. 'It will be my task to see that you improve it. My name is Raisa Nikitovna. Go to the last desk of the third row and sit down.'

Without another word, she picked up a book, and called out a page number. Everyone had a book but me. The feeling must have been something like being the only soldier without a gun. I leaned towards the girl next to me and asked if I might share her book. She **grudgingly** agreed. She was a very pretty girl with short blonde hair, and eyes the special blue of northern countries. I asked her name, but she told me to be quiet; there was absolutely no talking allowed in class.

My first lesson in school in Siberia was memorable for being a chilly one. It was not only the Russian author's meaning that **evaded** me, lost as it was in a sea of strange letters formed in the

Russian alphabet, but so did the book itself – literally. My classmate somehow managed to keep slipping it out of my field of vision, which forced me to strain, squirm, and nudge her to bring the book closer. Naturally, I had barely read the first paragraph when Raisa Nikitovna began to quiz the class. To my horror, one question was directed at me. As I began to answer in my halting Russian, all the children turned to stare at me.

When the lesson was finished, Raisa Nikitovna introduced me and said that I would share my books with Svetlana. Svetlana turned out to be the pretty girl sitting next to me; the prospect of sharing with her was not **heartening**. The more attention I got in class, the more she sulked. I sensed that Svetlana wanted to be the queen bee and that I had become her natural enemy. This was confirmed when I asked if I might come to her house and study with her. The answer was a sharp 'No!'. I would be allowed to go there to fetch books when she had quite finished with them, but otherwise I could jolly well trot home and study alone.

At the end of my first day at school, I went home and collapsed on the sofa. Out of the confusion of the day, three giants **emerged** to be slain: Svetlana, Raisa Nikitovna, and the Russian alphabet.

2
  a On a copy of Text 4A underline any unknown words to look up or ask the teacher.

  b Think of words of your own to describe Esther's first day at her new school. What words would you use?

  c Make a list of the experiences and feelings that caused Esther to go home and collapse.

  d Reread the first paragraph, about Esther waking up. What expectations does it raise for the reader?

  e Now reread the last paragraph. What is the effect on you as a reader?

3
  a Find the words in bold in Text 4A. Use them in sentences of your own which show their meaning.

  b Find the reported speech in the text. Change it to direct speech, giving Esther's and Svetlana's actual words.

  c Look at the last two sentences of the last-but-one paragraph, which are in reported speech. Why do you think Svetlana does not speak in direct speech, as the teacher does?

UNIT 4 School stories

Key point

Speech in stories

In narrative writing, using dialogue, i.e. conversation between characters, gives variety and drama to the telling of the story, and it also shows the relationship between the speakers. Sometimes reported, or indirect, speech is used to explain what a character said instead of direct speech. Reported speech is less immediate than direct speech, as it records what a person said in the past rather than in the present. We therefore need to make changes to what someone said when it becomes reported speech:

- The verb tense moves one step further towards the past. For example, 'They will get a prize' becomes *The teacher said that they would get a prize*.
- The first person (*I*) changes to the third person (*he* or *she*), and the second person (*you*) changes to the first person. For example, *She told me, 'You must come to the front of the class'* becomes *She told me I had to come to the front of the class*.
- Some place words change – *here* becomes *there* and *this* becomes *that*.
- Some time words change – *ago* becomes *before* (e.g. 'two days ago' → *two days before*) and *now* becomes *then*.

4 **a** Write one sentence each of your own words to describe the character of:
  i Esther **ii** the teacher **iii** Svetlana.

  b What do you think happens when Esther goes to school the following day, and how do you think she feels about it?

  c Write a continuation of the passage, of about half a page. Your writing should keep in character and follow the same style. Try to include some dialogue between Esther and Svetlana or the teacher.

Key point

Fictionalised autobiography

Text 4A is an example of fictionalised autobiography. This means that although the events of the narrator's life are generally based on true experience, they are exaggerated to make them more dramatic and engaging. The emotional responses are also made more extreme, and speech is used to make the characters and encounters seem more vivid, although it is not likely that the writer would be able to remember every word spoken in a conversation which took place many years before. See also the key point on autobiographical writing on page 12.

Text 4B

In this extract from *Cider with Rosie*, Laurie Lee gives a snapshot of his first day at a village school.

The morning came when my sisters surrounded me, wrapped me in scarves, tied up my bootlaces, thrust a cap on my head, and stuffed a baked potato in my pocket.

'What's this?' I said.
'You're starting school today.'
'I ain't. I'm stopping 'ome.'
'You are.'
'Boo-hoo.'

I arrived at the school just three feet tall and fatly wrapped in my scarves. **The playground roared like a rodeo** and the potato burned through my thigh. Old boots, ragged stockings, torn trousers and skirts, went sailing and skidding around me. The rabble closed in; I was encircled; **grit flew in my face like shrapnel**. Tall girls with frizzled hair, and huge boys with sharp elbows, began to prod me with hideous interest. They plucked at my scarves, **spun me round like a top**, screwed my nose and stole my potato.

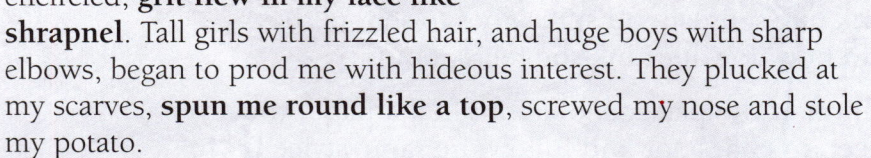

5 a In pairs, decide how Text 4B is similar to and different from Text 4A. Make notes on the situation, the narrator, the setting, the atmosphere and the language in both texts. You could use a table like the one on the next page to organise your notes in your notebook.

UNIT 4 School stories

	Similarities	Differences
Situation		
Narrator		
Setting		
Atmosphere		
Language		

b Look at the similes in Text 4B, which are in bold. Copy and complete each one using an image of your own.
  i The playground roared like . . .
  ii Grit flew in my face like . . .
  iii They spun me round like . . .

c Collect all your ideas together. Decide with the class which are the best substitute similes, and why. Now compare them with the ones in the text and discuss which are better, and why.

6 Draw this comic strip in your notebook. What could go in the empty frames? Complete the last four frames by drawing simple stick figures and giving them speech in bubbles, as in the first two.

Get out your homework please!

Sorry Miss, but something happened to it.

7 When you wrote the speech bubbles in the last activity, you did not have to think about using correct punctuation around the speech because it was in a comic strip. In story writing, however, you do need to use speech marks. In this activity, you will be looking at the direct speech in Text 4B and how it is punctuated.

  a In pairs, study the dialogue in Text 4B and notice how it is set out and punctuated. In pairs, decide on what you think are the rules for how direct speech is presented within a narrative.

  b Rewrite the dialogue in Text 4B as reported speech, inserting the necessary speakers and verbs. Remind yourself of the rules by looking back at the key point on speech in stories on page 43.

c   Now imagine that there is more dialogue in Text 4B. Imagine that:
   i   one of Laurie's sisters told him he needed to go to school to learn things
   ii Laurie replied that he could learn things by playing in the garden
   iii his mother told him that he would be late if he didn't hurry up.

Write the direct speech. Look at the key point about the position of the speaker in direct speech and include examples of all three possible positions in your sentences – before the speech, in the middle of the speech, and after the speech.

Key point

Speaker position in direct speech

- The speaker can be given first, before the speech, to introduce it: *She explained, 'I will do it later, when I've finished my work.'*
- Alternatively, the speaker can be given after the speech: *'I will do it later, when I've finished my work,' she explained.*
- Direct speech can also be split, with the speaker given in the middle of the speech: *'I will do it later,' she explained, 'when I've finished my work.'*

Text 4C

What is a teacher?

To a mind of flint, the teacher must be iron, and strike sparks. To the empty pitcher, the teacher becomes a well. To the fallow mind, a planter of seeds. To the cluttered mind, a gardener to weed, shape, and clear a space for growing.

To the lens, the teacher is light, and to the mind of light, a lens. To the sleeper, the teacher is the wake-up call of birds at sunrise. To clay, the teacher is potter, sculptor, and trainer in self-shaping. To the wanderer, the teacher is a knowing guide. To the developed mind, the teacher is colleague, listener, friend.

To all, the teacher is a mirror that shows not only the self but the path and its choices, the task and its demands – the difficulties, the joys. To all and from all, the teacher is a learner, a person – and a prism through which the ordinary continuously reveals itself to be miraculous.

Gerald Grow

UNIT **4** School stories

8 **a** Look up the definition of the word *teacher* in a dictionary. Do you think it conveys enough meaning or is there something missing? What would you add to it, if anything?

b Look at Text 4C, which is a collection of figurative definitions of a teacher. Read the text then think of some other metaphors and similes which you would use to define a teacher.

c Now write your own piece in the same format as Text 4C, beginning each sentence with 'To . . .'

Text 4D

First day at school

A millionbillionwillion miles from home
Waiting for the bell to go. (To go where?)
Why are they all so big, other children?
So noisy? So much at home they
Must have been born in uniform
Lived all their lives in playgrounds
Spent the years inventing games
That don't let me in. Games
That are rough, that swallow you up.

And the railings.
All around, the railings.
Are they to keep out wolves and monsters?
Things that carry off and eat children?
Things you don't take sweets from?
Perhaps they're to stop us getting out
Running away from the lessins. Lessin.
What does a lessin look like?
Sounds small and slimy.
They keep them in the glassrooms.
Whole rooms made out of glass. Imagine.

I wish I could remember my name
Mummy said it would come in useful.
Like wellies. When there's puddles.
Yellowwellies. I wish she was here.
I think my name is sewn on somewhere
Perhaps the teacher will read it for me.
Tea-cher. The one who makes the tea.

Roger McGough

9 a In pairs, look at the use of apostrophes in the poem in Text 4D and in the dialogue in Text 4B. How are they being used?

b Text 4D is a poem written by an adult but from the viewpoint of a child starting school. Make a list of the ways in which you think the child's viewpoint is shown in the poem (see the key point on page 8).

c Add some more observations and reflections that you think the child in the poem might have made while standing in the playground before going into school for the first time – about the teachers on duty, the kind of games being played, the uniform, for example. You can play with word sounds and make up words too, as the poem does.

Key point

Apostrophe of omission

Texts 4B and 4D both contain contractions. It is common in informal dialogue between people who know each other well for contracted verb forms to be used, to reflect the way we speak rather than the way we write, especially if it is a child speaking. It is usually the verbs *is* and *has* which are contracted (e.g. *he's, she's*), or other parts of the verb *be* or *have* (e.g. *I'm, we've*). The negative marker *not* is regularly reduced to *n't* (e.g. *it isn't, you hadn't*). The one or more letters which have been removed in a contracted form are indicated by an apostrophe. Sometimes missing letters and an apostrophe show dialect or regional forms of pronunciation, as in the case of *'ome* in Text 4B, which shows that Laurie pronounces *home* without the 'h' sound.

Text 4E

The writer Roald Dahl attended a boarding school and looked forward to going home for the vacations. This is an extract from his autobiography *Boy*.

> Towards the end of December, my mother came over on the paddle-boat to take me and my trunk home for the Christmas holidays. Oh the bliss and wonder of being with the family once again after all those weeks of fierce discipline! Unless you have been to boarding-school when you are very young, it is absolutely impossible to

UNIT 4 School stories

appreciate the delights of living at home. It is almost worth going away because it's so lovely coming back. I could hardly believe that I didn't have to wash in cold water in the mornings or keep silent in the corridors, or say 'Sir' to every grown-up man I met, or get flicked with wet towels in the changing-room, or eat porridge for breakfast that seemed to be full of little round lumpy grey sheep-droppings, or walk all day long in perpetual fear of the long yellow cane that lay on top of the corner-cupboard in the Headmaster's study.

10
  a Read Text 4E and summarise in one sentence why Roald Dahl did not like being at his boarding school.

  b In pairs, discuss and make notes on how contrast is used to create the setting and atmosphere of school in this passage.

  c List the details which are effective in making the school seem unpleasant.

11 Imagine that you are Roald Dahl at his boarding school. Write a letter home to an adult in your family, of about one page, saying how much you are looking forward to going home for the holidays. Look at the tip about writing a semi-formal letter before you start. In your letter:
- expand on the ideas in Text 4E, developing them with further details of your own
- include references to teachers and other students
- say what you are looking forward to enjoying when you get home.

Tip

For Activity 11
Semi-formal letter writing

Although you are writing to someone in your family, you will not speak to them in the way you would to a friend your own age. Try not to be too complaining or emotional, as you do not wish to upset them or give the impression that school is completely unbearable. You may therefore wish to use a light-hearted tone, as Roald Dahl does in Text 4E when he calls the porridge 'sheep-droppings'. Letters of this kind are usually a mixture of reflections, descriptions and references to events.

Text 4F

Monday: Hurray, end of term tomorrow! Can't wait for the holidays to start so that I can forget all about school and homework and just do what I want every day, get up when I like, and eat when I like. I'll spend the first day riding my bike or I'll go and visit my cousins. I know I'll get bored after a few days, but until then I am going to play, play, play.

Tuesday: Last day was fun; we had a party and played games and watched DVDs in lessons. Then something terrible happened at the end of the day: our form teacher gave us a sheet of homework assignments to be done over the holidays! I can't believe how long the list is. Sometimes I really don't like teachers!

Wednesday: Had to get up at the same time as usual, so that I could get some reading done before going out to play. I wish I was still in primary school. My little sister and brother don't get any homework so their holidays really are holidays!

UNIT 4 School stories

12 a Read Text 4F. What do you notice about the kind of sentences used in diary entries? Why do you think long and complex sentences are not normally used?

b Imagine that you have just been told that you can't go home from school today. The school has been put into a week's quarantine (isolated to prevent the spread of disease) because a student has been diagnosed with an infectious illness. Make some notes of your immediate thoughts and feelings.

c Write a diary entry, of about a page, to reflect how you feel about this situation.
  i Give your reflections about not being able to go home.
  ii Predict what you think is going to happen during the coming week.
  iii Describe some fellow students and teachers, and how they are reacting.

Key point

Writing a diary

Diary style consists of either simple sentences (sentences containing one verb) or compound sentences (ones which use *and, but, so* and *or* to connect verbs). This makes the writing seem simple and even childlike, but as you usually write a diary for yourself, there is no need to use complex grammar; the aim is simply to record what happened and what you thought and how you felt about it. Diary entries:
- include a mixture of narrative, description and reflection
- are written from the viewpoint of the first person, using the pronoun *I*
- refer to events that have happened recently
- refer to the people in the diary writer's life, and what they have said and done
- reveal the writer's secrets, hopes and fears
- contain direct speech to record dramatic or important utterances.

13 a Think about all the texts you have read in this unit and decide on an idea for a story about school. It could be a 'first day' memory, or a story about any event which happened in or around school. Decide whether it will be a sad or an amusing story.

b Plan your story. Use the tip about planning to help you.

c Now draft your piece of writing. It should be about two pages. Look at the key point on narrative writing on the next page to help you.

Tip

For Activity 13b
Planning a story

- Make a spider diagram, mind map or flow chart to organise the ideas you will use to create the plot and atmosphere of your story. It is important to know before you start writing your story how it is going to end, so make sure you know where your story is going.
- Decide on the characters and setting, and make notes next to them of some details which you can use to describe them.
- Finally, write some direct speech for some of the characters in your story to say.

Key point

Narrative writing

Many stories are based on a real incident which the writer has turned into an amusing or emotional experience. Bear the following points in mind when writing your own stories.

- You can build your story around something which did actually happen to you, or to someone you know. Alternatively, you could choose something you have read about as the basis of your story. In either case, exaggerate the incident to make it more amusing or dramatic.
- It is not a good idea to try to include a lot of characters or events in a story of a few pages. Select and focus on two or three of each, with one main one.
- Strong emotion will engage the reader, so consider using fear or confusion as the feeling in the story. To create the right atmosphere, choose appropriate vocabulary to match the feeling. It is better not to try to mix comic with serious.
- Consider the viewpoint. You can use first person (*I*) or third person (*he* or *she*), but you need to think what difference your choice will make. The emotion can be more powerful when *I* is used, as this gives the impression it is a true account and makes the reader sympathetic (as you saw in Text 4A). On the other hand, the writer can tell us more about what is going on in the heads of all the other characters if the third person is used, as in 'The teacher thought he looked lost and lonely, and felt sorry for him'.

UNIT 4 School stories

- The simplest narrative openings begin with a description of the setting or a character, so you could describe the building first, or you could start by describing a particular character before going on to describe the place.
- Include dialogue at the key moments in your story, as direct speech will help to convey the characters, and also to add drama. For a more subtle effect or for variety, use some reported speech as well as or instead of direct speech.
- Your story will be more effective if it has a strong ending, so think carefully about your last sentence and how to make it sound final.

UNIT 5 Up in the air

In this unit you will reflect on the things that you see in the air above you. You will have the opportunity to do some more summarising, paraphrasing and vocabulary building, as well as practising sequencing and paragraphing, sentence separation and use of commas.

Activities

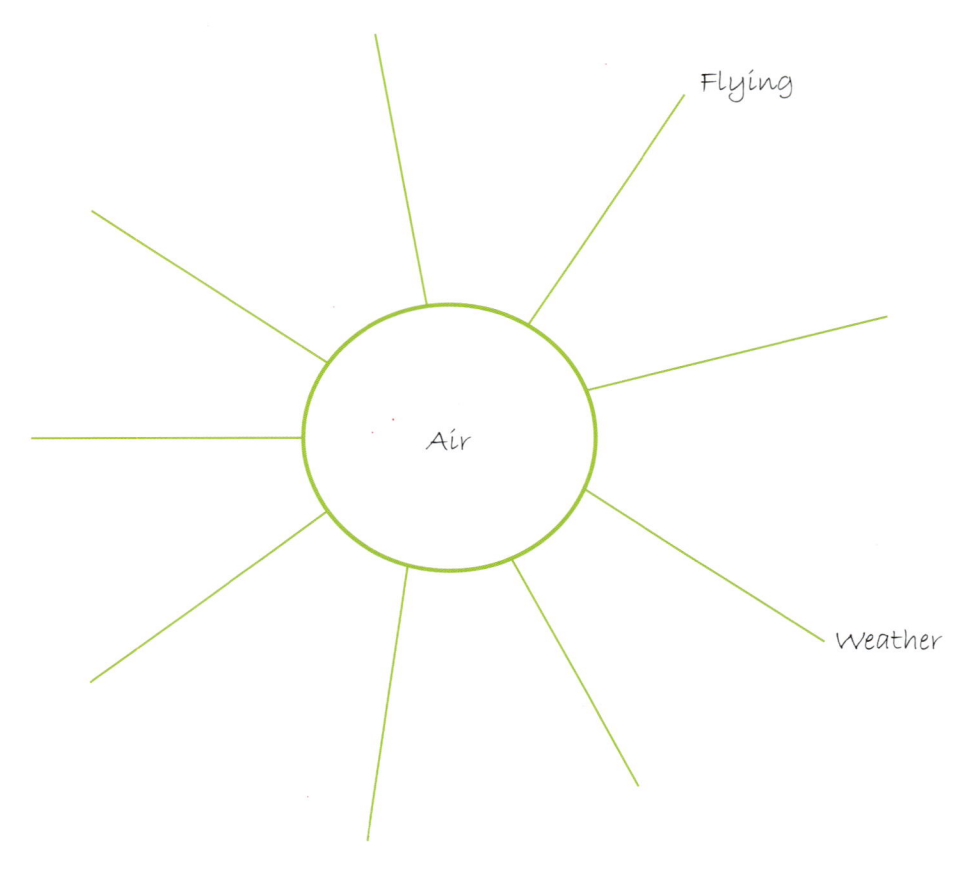

1

[Spider diagram with "Air" in the centre, with branches labelled "Flying" and "Weather"]

a Make a spider diagram for the word 'Air', collecting all the things you can think of which depend on or take place up in the air, and all the things you associate with it.

b Now organise your spider diagram into a mind map of related ideas, and give each group a subheading, such as 'Weather' and 'Flying'.

c Make a list of all the different types of weather and sky effects, for example hurricanes, rainbow, sunset.

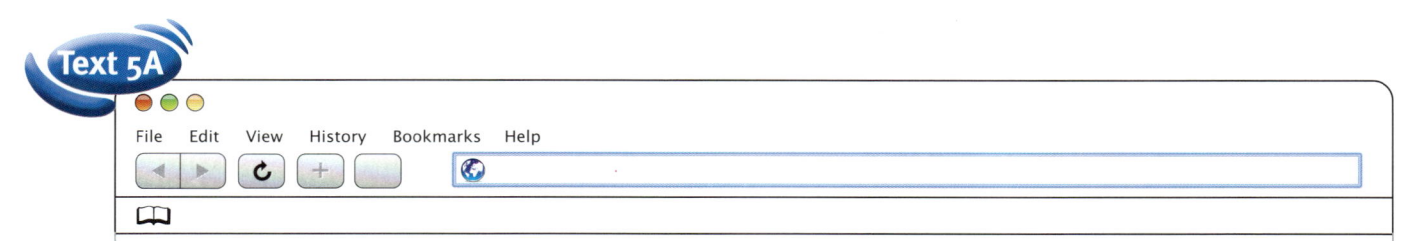

Kites

Kites were used **approximately** 2800 years ago in China, where materials **ideal** for kite building were readily available: silk fabric for the sail material; fine, strong silk for the flying line; and **resilient** bamboo for the lightweight framework. Ancient and medieval Chinese sources list the use of kites for measuring distances, testing the wind, lifting men, signalling, and communication for military operations. The earliest known Chinese kites were flat (not bowed) and often rectangular. Later, tail-less kites were developed. Kites were decorated with mythological **motifs** and legendary figures; some were fitted with strings and whistles to make musical sounds while flying.

After its introduction into India, the kite further **evolved** into the fighter kite known as the *patang* in India, and annual kite running competitions are held every year on the day of Makar Sankaranti. In Afghanistan, kite running is an ancient tradition, and it is **regarded** as an art as well as a sport; the aim of the kite runners is to cut the string of the kites belonging to their **opponents** with the string of their own. It is exciting and fun, but can also be dangerous, as kite runners can fall or run into things while they are involved in mid-air duels with rivals.

The period from 1860 to about 1910 was the golden age of kiting. Kites started to be used for scientific purposes, especially those to do with weather **forecasting** and photography; reliable manned kites were developed, as well as power kites. Then the invention of the powered aeroplane **diminished** the interest in kites, and since then they have been used mainly for **recreation**. You can see them being flown every evening in Tiananmen Square in Beijing, nearly three thousand years after they were first invented, in all shapes and forms, including eagles.

However, children nowadays do not fly kites as much as in previous times. The rival attractions of computer games have reduced the appeal of all outdoor activities, and there are fewer large spaces where kite flying can safely be done, thanks to the increase in the number of tall buildings and overhead power cables in so many countries.

2 a Think of four short subheadings which you could add to Text 5A, one before each of the four paragraphs, to summarise its content. Write the subheadings in your notebook.

b Look at the ten words in bold in the passage. Which words of similar meaning could you replace them with? You may need to use a thesaurus for this task. Write your replacement words in your notebook.

c Explain in your own words the meaning of the following phrases from Text 5A:
- duels with rivals
- the golden age
- thanks to the increase

3 For this activity, you need to find ideas in Text 5A to answer three specific questions. Select the points you would use in a summary about the following topics and list the points as brief notes.

a the building of kites

b the use of kites

c the history of kites

Key point

Selecting summary points

- Identify and underline the essential information needed to answer the question; do not include anything irrelevant, and ignore minor details, repetitions and examples.
- When you transfer the points to your own list or plan, change the phrases into your own words where possible, and try to reduce the number of words being used.
- Always paraphrase figurative language, such as 'the golden age of kiting' in Text 5A, to show that you have understood it.
- You may need to use the material in more than one part of the question, if it is relevant.

UNIT 5 Up in the air

Text 5B

9-year-old balloonist bids for record

A 9-year-old boy from Albuquerque, New Mexico, is preparing to make history by becoming the youngest trained pilot to fly solo in a hot air balloon. Bobby Bradley has been training for this moment since he was just 4 years old. He has more experience than some professional pilots, and admits that he's excited but not nervous about the prospect. He will take off in about 7 weeks' time.

Bobby's parents are Troy and Tami Bradley, who are well known in the ballooning community as two of the best in the world. They have won some of the biggest races ever staged, and Troy co-piloted the first ever balloon to journey from North America to Africa, making his first solo flight when he was 14.

Judging by interviews, young Bobby Bradley seems totally comfortable piloting the balloon and should have no problems. He says, 'I've always wanted to fly solo, and I've had plenty of time to train.'

4
  a Select the key points contained in the news report in Text 5B. Then reorganise the information into just one sentence in your notebook.

  b On a copy of the text, circle the commas used in Text 5B. Working in pairs, discuss and list the different purposes for which they are being used.

  c Read the key point about commas and then copy the following text into your notebook, adding the commas where necessary.

Although some wind is needed to fly hot air balloons they can't fly if there is too much wind. Balloons need cool stable calm winds to operate most effectively so early morning as the sun rises and when the winds are at their calmest is the best time. Also a lower temperature means it is easier to get the balloon off the ground without using so much gas and this means the balloon can be flown for longer.

Key point

Commas

Commas are needed within sentences to separate the items in a list or the different grammatical parts. You can choose whether to put a comma before a clause beginning with *and*, *but*, *so* and *or* (simple connectives), but usually we do put one if the sentence is already long, or if the new clause (a group of words containing a verb) is long, or if it contains a new idea.

UP, UP AND AWAY!

Let the breeze take you

Soar into the sky like an eagle in a Skycraft Hot-Air Balloon, and release your mind and spirit into the unlimited freedom beyond the horizon!

In a Skycraft you can fly over the Himalayas, or the valley of the sacred river Ganges, like gods! In a Skycraft you can see the earth beneath as you have never seen it before!

Let the snow-capped summits of majestic mountains take your breath away. Move silently through mist as though time has stopped. Experience sunrises and sunsets of unbelievable splendour.

Take the ultimate, unforgettable trip of a lifetime! Call Skycraft today, book a balloon ride, and change your life!

UNIT 5 Up in the air

5 Working with a partner, analyse the advertising language used in Text 5C.

   a In one sentence only, summarise the idea being offered to the customer by Skycraft balloons.

   b Define the type of sentences being used in this advert, and think of some reasons why this type of sentence is used in advertising.

   c Find all the examples of alliteration (words beginning with the same letter). What do you think is the reason for and effect of using alliteration in advertising?

   d Look at the use of exclamation marks. Why do you think there are so many, and what is the intention of the writer in using them?

   e Comment on the use of the following adjectives in the advertisement, and on their combined effect:
   - unlimited
   - unbelievable
   - unforgettable

   f Write another sentence to add to the advertisement. Explain why you have chosen this sentence.

Tip

For Activity 5f
Using advertising language

The most important thing about advertising language is that it must appeal to its audience. This can be achieved by arousing feelings of desire and envy in the reader, to make them want to do or have whatever is on offer. One of the ways to do this is to use evocative words and imagery, and another is to use memorable phrases that stick in the mind because of their sound. Advertisements do not aim to use original language or to avoid repetition of words; they want the reader to immediately recognise the idea and not have to think about what the language means. Repetition is actually desirable because it reinforces the message, and short slogans, simple sentences and clear layout guarantee immediate understanding.

Cambridge Checkpoint English 7

Text 5D

Seagull 1

Text 5D is from the novel *Jonathan Livingston Seagull* by Richard Bach.

It was morning, and the new sun sparkled gold across the ripples of a gentle sea. A mile from shore a fishing boat chummed the water, and the word for Breakfast Flock flashed through the air, till a crowd of a thousand seagulls came to dodge and fight for bits of food. It was another busy day beginning. But way off alone, out by himself beyond boat and shore, Jonathan Livingston Seagull was practising. A hundred feet in the sky he lowered his webbed feet, lifted his beak, and strained to hold a painful hard twisting curve through his wings. The curve meant that he would fly slowly, and now he slowed until the wind was a whisper in his face, until the ocean stood still beneath him. He narrowed his eyes in fierce concentration, held his breath, forced one … single … more … inch … of … curve … Then his feathers ruffled, he stalled and fell. Seagulls, as you know, never falter, never stall. To stall in the air is for them disgrace and it is dishonour. But Jonathan Livingston Seagull, unashamed, stretching his wings again in that trembling hard curve – slowing, slowing, and stalling once more – was no ordinary bird. Most gulls don't bother to learn more than the simplest facts of flight – how to get from shore to food and back again. For most gulls, it is not flying that matters, but eating. For this gull, though, it was not eating that mattered, but flight. More than anything else, Jonathan Livingston Seagull loved to fly. This kind of thinking, he found, is not the way to make one's self popular with other birds. Even his parents were dismayed as Jonathan spent whole days alone, making hundreds of low-level glides, experimenting.

6 a While reading Text 5D, pick out any words you don't know to ask your teacher. First try to guess their meaning by thinking about other words the unknown word reminds you of, or the meaning of the rest of the sentence.

b Text 5D needs to be paragraphed. There should be five paragraphs. On a copy of the text show by using the symbol // where you think the paragraph breaks should be, and think of the reasons for your decisions.

c Check with a partner to see if you have put them in the same places. If not, reconsider or argue for your choices.

Key point

Paragraph changes

A change of topic, time, place or action is usually the reason for starting a new paragraph. Sometimes a single sentence can be a paragraph, if it is the first or last one in a passage, or there is a need to create a dramatic effect, such as surprise or swift movement. When you do your own writing, you can always use the // symbol to show where you later think you should have started a new paragraph, so you can put these in when checking your work. In a piece of writing written by hand, a new paragraph is shown by starting the line further in than the margin. In typed text, however, the paragraph break may be shown without an indentation but with a blank line instead.

Text 5E

Seagull 2

In Text 5E, a lonely seagull has not yet learnt to fly.

The young seagull was alone on his ledge his two brothers and his sister had already flown away the day before he had been afraid to fly with them somehow when he had taken a little run forward to the brink of the ledge and attempted to flap his wings, he became afraid the great expanse of sea stretched down beneath, and it was such a long way down, miles down, he felt certain that his wings would never support him, so he bent his head and ran away back to the little hole under the ledge where he slept at night.

Even when each of his brothers and his little sister whose wings were far shorter than his own ran to the brink flapped their wings and flew away he failed to muster up courage to take that plunge which appeared to him so desperate. His father and mother had come around calling to him shrilly scolding him threatening to let him starve on his ledge unless he flew away but for the life of him he could not move.

That was twenty-four hours ago since then nobody had come near him the day before all day long he had watched his parents flying about with his brothers and sister perfecting them in the art of flight teaching them how to skim the waves and how to dive for fish he had in fact seen his older brother catch his first herring and devour it standing on a rock while his parents circled around raising a proud cackle and all the morning the whole family had walked about on the big plateau midway down the opposite cliff laughing at his cowardice.

From His First Flight *by Liam O'Flaherty*

7 In Text 5E some full stops and commas are missing. On a copy of the text:
- put the four missing full stops back into the first paragraph
- put the seven missing commas back into the second paragraph
- put the full stops *and* commas back into the third paragraph.

Text 5F

The Black Eagle

- The Black Eagle is a bird of prey, like all eagles.
- It soars over the forests of the hilly regions of tropical Asia.
- It hunts mammals on the ground, and birds and their eggs in nests.
- It is found in the Himalayan foothills of Nepal, India, and Sri Lanka.
- It is about 75 centimetres in length.
- Adults are black with a yellow bill and feet.
- They are easily identified by their splayed primary feathers, which form a characteristic silhouette.
- They fly slowly, often in a wheeling pattern, as they look for prey below.
- Their long claws are less strongly curved than those of other birds of prey.
- They can stay aloft for very long periods of time.
- They lay one or two white eggs with brown and mauve blotches.
- The Indian Giant Squirrel is one of its favourite prey.

UNIT 5 Up in the air

- They build a platform nest about one metre wide in a tall tree overlooking a steep valley.
- Their nesting season is between January and April. They often re-use the same nest.

8 Working with a partner, produce a leaflet on the Black Eagle.

a On a copy of Text 5F put numbers against the information bullets to show the order in which you will use them, and then type or write them out in sequence.

b Decide on sub-headings under which to group the different types of information about the eagle (for example, 'What they eat') and put them in the right places in your list.

c Design the leaflet (consisting of a folded sheet of blank A4 paper) and include some illustrations. These could be of the bird in flight, its nest, its habitat, or a map of the region. You can use colours, borders, boxes and different letter sizes and fonts. You could design your leaflet using a computer and print it out to be displayed in your classroom.

Text 5G

On Eagle's Wings

This is a fable inspired by the tales of the Kwaaymii Indians.

Long ago, before Eagles were chiefs of people, Grandmother Eagle was warming her feathers near Inya, the Sun. Down she gazed with sharp eyes, spying Kwinyaw, the Rabbit, who hopped to and fro.

'I am hungry,' Grandmother Eagle said. She folded her wings and swooped from near Inya, the Sun, and upon Kwinyaw. Before she opened her claws to snatch her prey, a baby Kwinyaw, as she had never seen before, scampered from the bushes.

Grandmother Eagle alighted beside Kwinyaw and said, 'What is that?'

Kwinyaw, seeing that Grandmother Eagle had decided not to eat her, responded, 'This is my child'.

'Where did he come from?'

'I dug him from the ground'. (For, in those days, children were not born, but sprang in infancy from the soil and water.)

'Where may I find a child of my own?' Grandmother Eagle asked.

'I do not know,' answered Kwinyaw, thumping her hind legs. 'Ask Inya, the Sun.'

As Grandmother Eagle warmed her feathers, Inya, the Sun, bade her fly low over the spring of Ah-ha' Kwe'se-i, and there she would find her child.

Speeding toward the spring of Ah-ha' Kwe'se-i, she dove low over the enchanted pool, and there was her son floating on its limpid pureness. Smiling as never before, Grandmother Eagle lifted him from Ah-ha' Kwe'se-i, and carried him to her nest upon the cliffs of the Ah-ha' Kwe-ah-mac', far above the stone fangs which loomed sharply from the mountain base.

She said to her son, 'I will call you Kwaaypaay, for you will be chief of people'.

Off Grandmother Eagle flew, picking food for her son. At first, she chose small creatures, but he grew and she fed him larger and larger prey.

One day, Grandmother Eagle alighted above him, and asked him to join her in a visit to Inya, the Sun. Alas, as always, Kwaaypaay refused and squeaked for more food.

Grandmother Eagle began to worry. 'He depends on me for everything. Gladly I provide. But he refuses to venture into the wide world beyond the Ah-ha' Kwe-ah-mac'. He will never fly high enough to warm his feathers beside Inya, the Sun.'

Grandmother Eagle decided to show her son the wide world beyond the Ah-ha' Kwe-ah-mac'. Pointing toward the southernmost Coyote Mountains, she said, 'There is where crafty

Huta-pah' ate the heart of his father. The blood fell to the ground, staining the dirt a ruddy hue'.

Kwaaypaay stepped near the edge of the nest curiously. His sharp eyes squinted into the distance, and he spied the dark sands. Satisfied, he slid back and yawned.

Grandmother Eagle said, 'Do you not wish to visit this place?'

'My eyes are sharp. I can see the wide world beyond the Ah-ha' Kwe-ah-mac' from here. You care for me, and I am comfortable.'

Grandmother Eagle pointed toward the evening home of Inya, the Sun. 'There lies the foggy shores of the great water.'

Kwaaypaay squinted from the edge of the nest toward the cool waters. As he watched, Grandmother Eagle pushed him over the edge, and he plunged out.

He squeaked his shock as he fell, but only the craggy rocks could hear him, and they simply shook their heads. His sharp eyes showed him the stone fangs at the mountain base, and he cried all the more, flapping his wings in futility, for he'd never used them before this very moment.

He closed his eyes, sure that the stone fangs at the mountain base would devour him, but Grandmother Eagle wrapped her talons around his body, and lifted him upward toward the safety of his nest.

* * * * *

The next day, Grandmother Eagle fed her son a long-tailed mouse. 'I snatched her from Nim-me', the wildcat, who growled in pain from the whip of Seen-u-how' which marked her coat.' Grandmother Eagle pointed, 'See where ice grows, well before the long fingers of winter reach us here.'

Kwaaypaay gazed out from the edge of the nest. Grandmother Eagle put her nose against his back and pushed him out.

Down he fell, squeaking as before, the craggy rocks again shaking their heads. He flapped his wings, but the wind passed through his feathers uselessly.

His strength gave out, and hope fled as he was nearly upon the stone fangs at the mountain base. A shadow passed over, and Grandmother Eagle snatched him from very teeth that would devour him.

'Why do you push me over the edge?' Kwaaypaay asked.

'So you will learn,' Grandmother Eagle answered.

'But surely I will be killed.'

'You have not been killed yet. For my eyes are sharp, and I watch you.'

Kwaaypaay yawned in exhaustion and fell asleep.

Grandmother Eagle woke him, 'There, toward the morning home of Inya, the Sun, lies Water in Rock, warm springs welling from desert sands.'

Kwaaypaay lazily stepped to the edge of the nest, feeling the familiar push against his back before he plunged out.

He cried and flapped. The craggy rocks shook their heads. And just as he was sure to be destroyed, Grandmother Eagle grasped him gently and lifted him away.

* * * * *

How many days this went on, only the stones know. But one day, as Kwaaypaay plunged toward the stone fangs at the mountain base, he caught a draft within his feathers. It slowed his fall. He flapped again, harder now, and behold, he halted his fall.

Grandmother Eagle swooped down, calling, 'Glide over here'.

He spread his wings, cupping the wind beneath his feathers, and glided toward Grandmother Eagle. An updraft caught him and lifted him until he was soaring above the nest.

'Come,' Grandmother Eagle called from within the nest, 'let us eat together'.

Kwaaypaay shook his head and circled. 'No. I have spent enough days in the nest. I want to warm my feathers beside Inya, the Sun, and venture into the wide world beyond the Ah-ha' Kwe-ah-mac'.'

Grandmother Eagle was proud and happy, for she knew that Kwaaypaay would truly be chief of people.

Mark S. Bubien

9 a Explain these verbs in your own words (or look them up in a dictionary if you are not sure of the meaning):
- swoop
- scamper
- squint
- glide
- gaze
- snatch
- soar
- spy

b What is the moral of the legend in Text 5G?

c Paraphrase (use your own words) and summarise the story by reducing it to half a page of writing, leaving out details and anything else which is not strictly necessary for the narrative. Consider where to start new paragraphs.

UNIT **5** Up in the air

Tip

For Activity 9c
Summarising

Traditional tales – folk legends, fairy tales and fables – typically have a structure of things happening three times, so that suspense is created and the lesson is fully learned. When you are summarising a story you do not need to say what happens every time an event is repeated. Tales also often include dialogue, which is not needed in a synopsis (summary) of the plot. Some of the description and naming of people and places can also be reduced or removed, to allow you to focus on what actually happens in the story.

10 To finish this unit, you will use ideas you have come across during the previous activities to give a talk to the class.

  a Choose one weather type and collect a list of vocabulary which is relevant to a description of it, e.g. *sparkling* for *frost*, *blazing* for *sunshine*. You can use a thesaurus to find longer, more interesting words to use in place of everyday ideas. For example, there are many more exciting words than *wet* or *hot*.

  b Think about what your chosen weather does, in terms of how the landscape and wildlife respond to it, and how it makes people feel when they look at it or are caught up in it. Describe what it's like to be both indoors and outdoors during this kind of weather. Add some images: 'A thunderstorm is like copper pans falling down stone steps', or 'A sunset is as colourful as an artist's palette', for example.

c Plan your talk, of about three minutes, on your chosen topic. Use the descriptive notes you have made, plus some extra reflections of your own from personal experiences and memories. You can also research and add quotations from poems, or statistics from factual sources of information. Practise your talk with a partner first, and get them to time you. Then you can add more ideas or get rid of the less effective ones, depending on the length.

d Give your talk, making sure that you speak slowly and clearly enough for your audience to be able to hear and understand everything you say. Try to put some intonation (expression and variety of tone) into your delivery.

e As you listen to the talks of the rest of the class, think how you would rate their talk, on a scale of 1–10. Take into account:
   - the interest and variety of the content (how engaging and wide-ranging are the ideas?)
   - the fluency and pace of the delivery (how well-connected is the talk, and is the speed appropriate?)
   - the clarity and expression of the voice (how clear is the pronunciation and how varied is the intonation?)

UNIT 6 Imaginary worlds

This unit looks at fantasy fiction, which includes magical events set in a historically distant or imaginary world of either the past or the future. Folk tales are traditional oral stories which contain legendary figures and exaggerated events. Science fiction is set in a future and more technologically advanced time. You will learn about story structure and story openings, and plot summaries. The language tasks will focus on relative clauses (introduced by *who* and *which*) and the use of past tenses.

Activities

1.
   a. Work in pairs to list the science fiction or fantasy stories in books and films that you can remember.

   b. Discuss in class what you think makes these types of unreal story so attractive to readers and viewers.

   c. Are any of the characters in these stories stereotypical? In other words, are any of them the easily recognisable characters often found in this sort of story, such as a lonely child who sees things others cannot see, or an alien visiting Earth? Make a list of the stereotypical characters which appear in more than one of the stories you thought of.

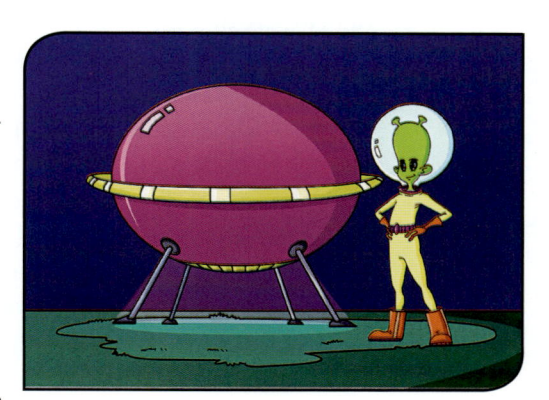

2. A cliché is a predictable idea, event or situation. Below is a list of some of the clichés found in fantasy and science fiction stories:
   - travelling back or forwards in time
   - arriving on a planet never before visited
   - moving to a new and strange house
   - having a dream which reveals something
   - being sent on a mission to defeat someone or something
   - being rescued at the last minute
   - discovering a code or secret
   - being misjudged and banished.

   a. Think of the titles of books, films or television programmes in which these ideas have featured.

   b. What do you think are the reasons for these typical events? Discuss as a class.

   c. Talk in pairs about fantasy and science fiction stories and think of some more clichés to add to the list.

Text 6A

The Messenger

This text is a traditional folk tale from South India.

The kingdom of Vijaynagar had not been enjoying good relations with its neighbouring state for a very long time. Jealous opponents of Tenali Rama, one of the king's ministers and the most able of them all, found it the perfect opportunity to damage his reputation. So they went about poisoning King Krishnadeva Rai's mind against him.

* * * * *

One day, when the king sat in his chamber pondering over the affairs of the state, one of his courtiers came up and whispered into his ear, 'Your Majesty, have you heard the latest?'

The king was surprised and exclaimed, 'No, I have not! What's going on?'

'Your Majesty, Tenali is in the pay of the neighbouring king. He has been spying on us for them.'

'What are you talking about?' asked the king angrily.

'This has been going on for a long time, your Majesty. But you would not listen to a word against Tenali. He has cast such a spell on you that you refuse to even think that he might betray you.'

'Tenali Rama is faithful to the kingdom. It is impossible that he would do such a thing. You have been misinformed,' the king replied with confidence.

But the courtier convinced the king to take his accusation seriously in those times of great intrigue. The king promised to investigate the matter and agreed that if Tenali Rama was found guilty, he would be punished. But his heart was heavy and he hoped that Tenali Rama would deny the charge.

* * * * *

The king sent for Tenali Rama the following day. Without wasting time he immediately asked the minister whether he was in league with the neighbouring state.

The question shocked Tenali Rama so much that he could not say anything. When Krishnadeva Rai found that Tenali Rama had nothing to say, he became angry and thundered, 'Your silence shows your guilt.'

Deeply hurt that the king could doubt his loyalty, Tenali Rama said that he refused to answer such a preposterous charge. This made the king even more angry. He ordered Tenali Rama to leave his kingdom. He could have ordered him to be put to death for the crime of treachery, but the king respected Tenali Rama's high status and their previous good relationship.

UNIT 6 Imaginary worlds

Tenali Rama did not say a single word in his defence and went away with his head bowed in misery. When his enemies heard that Tenali Rama had been expelled from the kingdom, their joy knew no bounds.

* * * * *

Tenali Rama reached the neighbouring state and met the king there. When Tenali Rama revealed his name, the king welcomed him warmly. He had heard much about Tenali Rama's wisdom.

But the king was surprised to see Tenali Rama in his court. 'Raja Krishnadeva Rai considers me his enemy, so what are you doing here?'

The minister replied, 'Majesty, you are a learned man. You have great strength. You are a good administrator and wish your people well. Our king also possesses all these virtues. He regards you as a friend and he has sent me to remove the existing misunderstanding between us.'

The king was surprised. 'Your king considers me a friend? But our spies warned us that Krishnadeva Rai was thinking of attacking us.'

Tenali Rama said, 'Our spies have fed our king the same pack of lies. That is why he has sent me to you. Has war ever benefitted anybody?'

The king believed Tenali Rama's story. He said, 'I do not want war, either. But how can I believe that Krishnadeva Rai really wants peace?'

Tenali Rama suggested that the king send a messenger with gifts and a message of peace to Vijaynagar. If King Krishnadeva Rai accepted the gifts, it would mean that he, too, wanted to be friends. But if he returned the gifts, then obviously he wanted war.

The king was impressed with this idea, and sent his special messenger to Vijaynagar the next day.

* * * * *

Meanwhile, King Krishnadeva Rai had come to know that Tenali Rama was innocent and that the courtiers had conspired against him. As soon as the messenger from the neighbouring state reached him with costly gifts, he was delighted. He was full of praise for Tenali Rama's wisdom and sent his own minister with gifts to the neighbouring state, with a request that the king send back Tenali Rama.

When Tenali Rama returned to Vijaynagar, King Krishnadeva Rai welcomed him warmly and offered him precious gifts. He rewarded him with an even higher rank in the court, that of chief minister. And he also swore that he would punish the wicked courtiers who had poisoned his ear against his favourite.

Adapted from www.pitara.com

3 Working with a partner, make three lists:

  a of the characters in Text 6A, including examples of similar characters in other folk or fairy tales you have read of or seen as films

  b of the events in the story, giving examples of similar events which happen in other fantasy stories or plays

  c of any language used which reminds you of the vocabulary found in other folk and fairy tales.

4 There are five main stages to story-telling:
  1 setting
  2 character
  3 problem
  4 crisis
  5 resolution.

  a Discuss in class why these five elements are all necessary for a successful narrative.

  b Look again at Text 6A and identify the five narrative stages.

  c Think of another folk tale which you know. Copy the table below into your notebook and complete it with notes for each stage of the story.

Title of folk tale	
Setting	
Character	
Problem	
Crisis	
Resolution	

5 Imagine you are going to write a fantasy or science fiction novel. Follow the steps below and use the tip on the next page to help you.

  a First, decide on the type of story you want to write. To help you decide, look back at the list of clichés you made in Activity 2c and your lists of characters and events from Activity 3.

  b Make a plan for your storyline, using the five headings from Activity 4. Summarise what will happen in each stage of the story.

  c Now decide on more details about the setting, character and plot, and add them to each of the stages.

UNIT 6 Imaginary worlds

Tip

For Activity 5
Planning your story

- Choose **settings** which would be considered suitable for a sci-fi or fantasy story because they convey the appropriate futuristic or unreal atmosphere. Make sure you have mentioned *when* the story takes place (what historical period, and what time of year) and *where* (which country and what kind of location).
- Make sure your **characters** are recognisable types according to the expectations for this kind of narrative fiction.
- The **problem** is likely to be a family issue or an external threat.
- What brings a story to a **crisis** is a difficult decision or dangerous attempt which has to be made.
- The **resolution** is usually that everything turns out alright in the end, after the difficulties and dangers have been overcome. Because it is not possible to base a fantasy story on your own experience, you need to think carefully about how to make it sound convincing. Specific and descriptive details will help to achieve this.

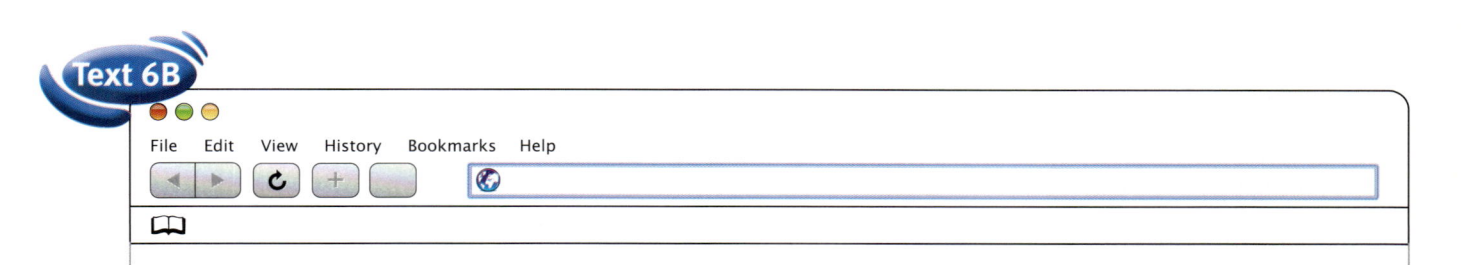

Text 6B

A science fiction synopsis

This story is set in the early 20th century near London. The narrator is not given a name. He witnesses the landing of a cylinder space ship. It was launched from Mars. It opens to let out tentacled Martians. They assemble strange machinery in the form of tripods. When humans move towards the Martians, they are incinerated by an invisible heat-ray. The narrator flees the scene. He meets a soldier. This man tells him a that another cylinder has landed. It cuts the narrator off from his wife.

These war machines defeat the army's weapons and start to attack the local communities. More cylinders land across the English countryside and people flee their homes in the face of the invasion. Three of the tripods are destroyed by the military, but soon all organised resistance has been overcome. A Martian red weed appears. It takes over the landscape. The narrator becomes trapped in a half-destroyed building. He sees the Martians from close by. They behave in a terrifying way towards the humans they catch. He only narrowly escapes capture himself.

In the end, both the red weed and the Martians themselves are defeated by bacteria. These do not exist on Mars and so have a fatal effect.

6 Text 6B is a synopsis of a science fiction story by H.G. Wells called *The War of the Worlds*. In this activity, you will look at plot summaries and relative clauses. Read the key point about relative clauses below to help you.

  a There are places in Text 6B where a relative clause beginning with *who* could have been used. For example, in the first paragraph it could have said: 'The narrator, who is not given a name, witnesses …' Find other examples of places where *who* could have been used.

  b There are also places in Text 6B where a relative clause beginning with *which* could have been used. For example, in the first paragraph it could have said: 'He witnesses the landing of a cylinder space ship, which was launched from Mars.' Find other examples of places where *which* could have been used.

  c Summarise the plot synopsis further by reducing it to only five sentences. Make sure you keep the essential information. You can also use compound connectives, but try to use relative pronouns where possible.

Key point

Relative clauses 1

Using *who* or *which* in a sentence is a way of adding extra information about someone or something, using another clause containing a verb. For example, in the sentence 'They cautiously opened the box, which had been locked for many years', the main clause contains the verb *opened*, and the relative clause contains the verb *had been locked*;

UNIT **6** Imaginary worlds

the relative clause begins with the relative pronoun *which*. The use of relative clauses avoids repeating the name of a person or thing, and it improves writing style by producing a more interesting sentence structure than is possible with simple sentences or compound sentences using *and*. You should try to use this way of joining parts of sentences in your own writing, as it is an important writing skill to be able to form longer and more varied sentences.

7   a   Write a plot synopsis of the story you planned in Activity 5, of about half a page. Note that we talk about fiction in the present tense, so we say, for example, *he meets*, not *he met*.

   b   Consider some titles of fantasy or science fiction novels and films. You can refer back to the titles you collected in Activity 1 and look at the tip below to help you. Discuss in class what they have in common as titles. After careful consideration, give your story a name.

   c   Look at some science fiction or fantasy book covers. Design a book cover for your novel. Think of a suitable illustration to represent what it is about. Also consider the use of colour, and the type of lettering – size and shape, capitals or small letters – for the title. Add your own name. Draw and colour, or design on a computer and print, a final version of the cover. This can be displayed on the wall of your classroom.

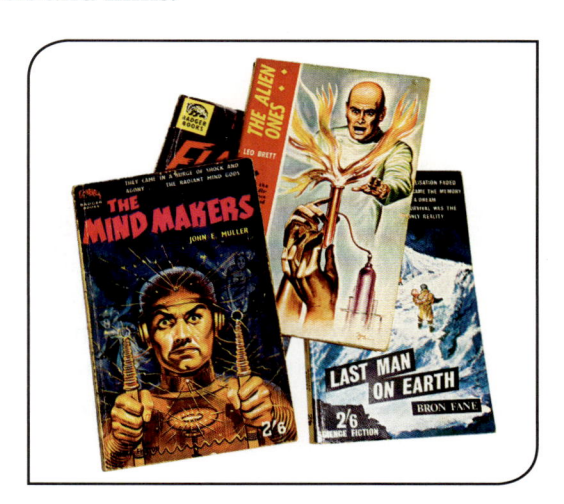

Tip

For Activity 7b
Choosing a title

Titles should not be long, usually no more than five words and often only one or two. They need to indicate what kind of story they refer to, so that readers or viewers know what genre (category of writing) they belong to. Good titles sound intriguing but do not give away exactly what will happen or what the outcome of the story will be, so 'The War of the Worlds' is better than 'A Martian Invasion' or 'The Defeat of the Martians'. It is also more memorable because it contains alliteration. (See also the tip on page 20 in Unit 2 about story titles.) Notice that in titles the nouns, adjectives and other important words have capital letters, but the grammar words (articles and prepositions) do not, except for the first word.

8 Read this typical blurb:

> Bilbo Baggins, a quiet and respectable hobbit, is paid a surprise visit by the wizard Gandalf, who offers him the chance to go on an adventure to the Lonely Mountain with thirteen dwarves to recover treasure guarded by Smaug the dragon. Bilbo accepts with uncharacteristic bravery and determination, both of which he will need on the long and challenging journey. But will he succeed?

Write a blurb for your novel after reading the tip.

Tip

For Activity 8
Writing a blurb

The aim of a blurb, printed on the back cover of a book, is to attract readers but without giving away exactly what will happen in the story or how it will end. It mentions the main characters and their general situation, and tries to make them sound interesting and exciting enough to arouse curiosity. Blurbs often end with a question mark or an ellipsis [...].

9 A tagline is a memorable phrase which sums up the idea a film is based on and which appears on publicity posters for the film. Below are the taglines for some well-known sci-fi films. Choose your favourite and explain why you think it was so successful in attracting people to see the film.
- You'll believe a man can fly!   *Superman*
- A long time ago, in a galaxy far, far away . . .   *Star Wars*
- To boldly go where no man has gone before.   *Star Trek*
- The truth is out there.   *The X-Files*
- We are not alone.   *Close Encounters of the Third Kind*

Imagine your novel is going to be made into a film. Write an interesting tagline to go on the poster to make the film sound exciting. Use the tip on the next page to help you.

UNIT **6** Imaginary worlds

Tip

For Activity 9
Writing a tagline

Consider how you will punctuate your tagline. Notice that some taglines are not completed with a full stop but end with an ellipsis [...], which creates mystery. Question and exclamation marks can also be used for effect (e.g. 'Is seeing really believing?'). Yet seemingly factual statements can sometimes be more intriguing, as in the example 'Nothing is what it seems'.

10 Read the key point about beginning stories and then practise these new types of story openings.

   a Write five opening lines for your fantasy story which start in the middle of a conversation in direct speech between two main characters.

   b Now write five opening lines for your fantasy story which start in the middle of an event or series of actions.

   c Exchange your openings with your partner, and discuss which would work better for the story you have planned, starting in the middle of the dialogue or starting in the middle of the action. Perhaps you will decide that neither of these types of beginning would be right for your story, and that a standard opening, describing character or setting, would be better; if so, say why.

Key point

Beginning stories

There are ways of beginning a story other than describing the setting or the characters. Stories can start, for example, in the middle of a speech:

> 'I think that's a completely mad idea and I refuse to have anything to do with it,' said my elder brother.

They can also start in the middle of the action:

> The time had come, and as the clock struck midnight, they put on their masks and the procession began to wind its way up the side of the cliff.

> These are effective ways of starting a story because they immediately involve readers by engaging their curiosity, making them want to find out who the people are and what has already happened.

Text 6C is a cutting from the book review page of a magazine. It is a review of a fantasy horror story.

Text 6C

★★★☆☆

Nightmare Attic by Amy Villiers is written in a rather old-fashioned style, which is traditional for horror stories set in the distant past but is not engaging for younger contemporary readers. Much of the dialogue is also awkward and entirely unnatural, and there's far too much of it. The book would also benefit from less description about the house and more information about its inhabitants, the living ones, as it's hard to identify with the family when we're told so little about them.

The line-up of supernatural characters and events include the usual favourites: ghosts, time travel, monsters in the attic, dead bodies bent on revenge, disappearing visitors, strange noises in the night. Though these are all predictable, there is enough going on to keep up the pace and provide variety. The temptation to pile on the gore has been resisted and, most importantly, the reader is kept guessing about the outcome of the story.

The author manages to build up suspense and the ending is worth waiting for. Those who enjoy classic horror and campfire ghost stories will certainly appreciate this addition to the genre.

11 First read the key point about quoting from texts to help you with this activity. Then quote from Text 6C the phrases that tell us:

a what makes a horror story successful

b what can be the weaknesses of a horror story

c what is unsatisfactory about the dialogue in the book being reviewed.

Key point

Use of quotation

When you are asked to quote evidence from a passage, as you are often asked to do in exam questions, you need to find exactly the right phrases, neither longer nor shorter than is necessary to answer

UNIT 6 Imaginary worlds

the question. Copy them accurately from the passage, putting them between inverted commas to show that they are quotations. The identified phrases can be given on their own as a list in short answer questions. Always look for *all* the possible evidence in a text rather than just the first one or two you find when you reread it. You need to copy punctuation accurately as well, if there is any included in your quotation. If you want to shorten a quotation by removing unnecessary words from the middle of it, you show that you have left out words by using this ellipsis sign [...] in place of the missing bit.

12 a Think of two characters in your story who would be likely to talk to each other in direct speech.

  b Think of the best time to use a piece of dialogue between the two characters, i.e. a dramatic moment in the action or at the climax of your story.

  c Write the dialogue which takes place between your chosen characters at your chosen moment. Try to make it sound natural by thinking about how people really speak to each other. Use the tip on dialogue in stories to help you.

Tip

For Activity 12c
Dialogue in stories

When people speak to each other in real life, they don't keep using each other's name. Too many repetitions of the characters' names is therefore a sign of unnatural dialogue in stories. If you set out your dialogue properly, you don't need to give the name of the speakers because after the first line the reader will understand that they are taking it in turn to speak.

Too much dialogue will turn your story into a play and reduce its effect as a narrative, so use it sparingly for important utterances at key moments.

In frightening or surprising situations, people do not normally speak at great length, but they do more than just make noises like 'Argh!' They usually manage to finish their sentence rather than just stop in the middle (represented by an ellipsis [...]). Also remember that, however exciting an event is, you should not use more than one question mark or exclamation mark. Noises like 'Eek!', dots and multiple question or exclamation marks are all features of comic strip speech, where there isn't room for many words in a speech bubble so punctuation is used rather than words to convey strong emotion.

13 Something which students often find difficult when writing narrative is the sequence of past tenses. There are four past tenses and students are often unsure which one to use in their sentences. Read the key point below about past tenses in stories before you do this activity.

  a Now write four separate sentences, one for each of the past tenses talked about in the key point, which show how each one is used.

  b Look again at the example in the key point below of a piece of writing containing all four past tenses. Write your own example sentence which includes all four past tenses.

  c Look back at the work you did on the opening of your story in Activity 10c. What type of beginning did you decide to write? Write your first three sentences. Check that they are in the appropriate tense or tenses. Read the key point below on narrative tense.

Key point

Past tenses in stories

- **Present perfect** – The present perfect is used when the action is not completed or when the time an action took place is not given (e.g. 'I have seen them before', 'he has almost finished').
- **Past simple** – The past simple is used when an action was completed at a specified or understood time (e.g. 'I did it yesterday evening').
- **Past perfect** – The past perfect is used when an action was completed before another action in the past (e.g. 'I had visited the house many times before the night I heard the strange noise in the attic').
- **Past continuous** – The past continuous is used for an action that was ongoing before it was interrupted by another action (e.g. I was watching television when there was a knock at the door').

This piece of writing contains all four of the past tenses: 'After I had investigated the room at the end of the corridor, I was feeling very frightened, so I ran away, and have never returned.'

Narrative tense

Some authors write narrative in the present tense, called the present historic, to give their story a sense of immediacy, and students often think that they can write their story in the present tense too. It is very difficult to remember to keep this up, however, and stories begun in the present nearly always switch to the past tense after a few lines, or they keep jumping between the two,

UNIT 6 Imaginary worlds

> which is confusing for the reader. It is more natural to start and stay in the past for an account of something which has already happened. Dialogue can be used to create a sense of the story happening now.

14 a You have now done a lot of preparatory work on your own fantasy or sci-fi story. Look back through your notes and plans, and use them to write the opening chapter for your novel, of about two pages.

b Swap drafts with your partner and act out being the teacher: say whether you are gripped and would want to read more, give advice on how it could be improved, and point out any errors of expression you have noticed.

c Write a final draft by hand or on a computer, and check it carefully before giving it to your teacher. Take note of the advice in the tip box to help you with your writing.

Tip

For Activity 14c
Common errors in narrative writing
Watch out for the following as you write your story.

Grammar errors
- 'Me and my friends' or 'I and my friends'. It should be *I* not *me*, because it is the subject of the verb, and it is not polite to put yourself first, so the correct expression is 'My friends and I'.
- Starting sentences with *And*, *But* and *So*. These are connectives to be used within compound sentences but they do not usually begin sentences.
- Forgetting that some plural nouns are irregular, e.g. *teeth* and *mice*, and that in nouns ending in a *y* which is pronounced as a syllable, e.g. *mystery*, the *y* changes to *ies* to make it plural: *mysteries*.
- Confusing *where / were / we're; there / their / they're; there's / theirs; your / you're; too / to / two*. Make sure you know the difference between these commonly confused words.
- Putting *this* before something you have not mentioned yet, such as 'and then we came across this house', or 'then this man suddenly appeared'.

Punctuation and presentation
- Forgetting to set out dialogue so it is clear who is speaking and which words are actually being spoken. Remember to start a new line for a change of speaker. Put thoughts in speech marks too, as these need to punctuated as well as words actually spoken out loud.
- Poor letter formation, e.g. writing *j* and *p* above the line instead of on the line.
- Wrong use of capitals, e.g. using a small *i* for *I*, using a capital letter for no reason, forgetting to give names of places a capital.
- Writing *a lot of*, *in front of* and *in fact* as one word, or writing *nevertheless* as three words and *indeed* as two words.

Vocabulary
- Using made-up words is not a good idea, even if they can be found in online dictionaries, e.g. *humongous* or *ginormous*, as these could make your story more comic than sinister.
- Certain adjectives (especially *nice*, *big*, *small*, *good* and *bad*) are too vague to give a clear picture to the reader and are best avoided. Use more precise descriptive words instead. Generally, words of more than one syllable are more interesting and evocative.

UNIT 7 Down to earth

In this unit you will be invited to think about your natural surroundings, your garden and what lives in it, as a stimulus for writing poems and personal accounts. You will practise your comprehension and vocabulary skills, learn more about commas, and look at prepositions.

Activities

1 a In your notebook, list the creatures which you find in and around your home, such as flies and squirrels. Write next to each whether they are an insect, mammal, rodent or reptile. You may need to check the definitions of these.

 b Underline in red the ones which you don't like and try to avoid, and underline in blue the ones which you don't mind or maybe even like.

 c Compare lists and preferences with the rest of the class, and discuss why some creatures are liked and others are disliked.

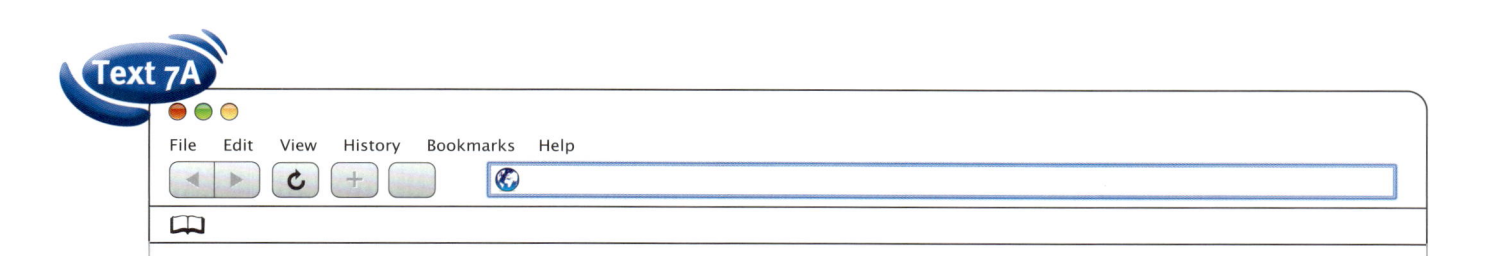

Text 7A

A rattling experience

There was a rattlesnake sunning itself on my back porch yesterday morning, a western diamondback about a metre long. I walked out there barefoot and half asleep, **clutching** coffee and newspapers, and almost stepped on its head. My right foot was beginning its blind descent when I heard the rattle, and, before my conscious brain had time to react, my body leaped back into the house and slammed the door. The snake, of course, was as **startled** as I was and beat a slithering retreat.

For the past two months I have lived on five acres of unfenced desert outside Tucson, Arizona. There are dozens of isolated houses dotted around but the land in between has been left largely **intact** since primeval times. Through my study window I have seen dozens of varieties of lizards; I have shaken a scorpion out of my shoe and chased a tarantula out of the kitchen.

But it's the rattlesnakes that dominate my perception of this landscape. Their venom, although **seldom** fatal to a healthy adult within reach of hospital, causes **excruciating** pain, sickness and permanent tissue damage. They won't bite unless severely provoked – or trodden on – but the threat never leaves one's mind. I am often asked why on earth I live in such a place, but I enjoy the presence of rattlesnakes and the wildness it implies.

At present, the rattlesnakes are preparing for hibernation and increasingly I am finding them in the house, attracted by the heat and the rodents that come here to gnaw, nest, burrow and steal my food. That is a little *too* close for comfort, but what to do?

In the absence of an ideal solution I now keep one or two rattlesnakes around and relocate the others. I fashioned a noose at the end of a long pole and snared a snake around its middle. It struck at the pole and I saw a blur of pink from its mouth and felt the sharp knock of its fangs against the wood. I lowered it into an ice chest and slammed the lid shut with the pole.

My plan was to release the snake in a beautiful canyon in the mountains where I camped last summer. I got there and found it had been bulldozed of its vegetation, closed to the public and littered with hideous condominiums and giant concrete carports. I let the snake go at the entrance gate.

Richard Grant

2 Read Text 7A. Using your own words, answer the following questions. Read the key point on answering comprehension questions to help you.

   a What happened when the writer heard the rattle of the snake, as described in paragraph 1?

   b Why do rattlesnakes bite and what are the effects, as described in paragraph 3?

   c How did the writer capture a snake, as described in paragraph 5?

UNIT 7 Down to earth

Key point

Answering comprehension questions

When you are asked to say what happens in a passage, it is your comprehension (understanding) which is being tested. If you simply repeat the words of the passage, you are not showing that you have understood its meaning, so that is why you must change as many of the words as possible into your own words when you give an answer. Use synonyms where you can, or at least change the order of the words where it is not possible to use different ones. Your paraphrase should not be any longer than the original phrases, and preferably a little more concise. Answer in full sentences, beginning with 'The writer . . . ' or 'This happens because . . . ', according to the way the question is phrased. Sometimes comprehension is tested by your being asked to select words from the passage which show something. Then you may answer by quoting phrases from the passage, using inverted commas to show your answer is a quotation. See the key point about the use of quotation on page 78 in Unit 6.

3 **a** Give synonyms for the five words in bold in Text 7A. You may need to use a thesaurus to help you. In each case, choose the word which fits best into the passage and is the right part of speech.

   b Find and quote the words in the passage which mean:

downward movement	way of seeing
aware	long-lasting
sliding	seriously
ancient	made angry
govern	winter sleep

   c On a copy of Text 7A, circle all the uses of *its* and *it's* in the passage. With a partner, work out what it means in each case, and the rule for when it does and doesn't need an apostrophe. Then write two sentences, one containing *its* and one containing *it's*.

4 On your copy of Text 7A, circle in a different colour the commas in the first paragraph of the passage. Work out with a partner the three different ways they are being used. Use the key point on using pairs of commas on the next page to help you, and also look back at the key point on commas on page 57 in Unit 5. Now write out and complete the following statements:

   a The first use of commas is to . . .

   b The second use of commas is to . . .

   c The third use of commas is to . . .

Cambridge Checkpoint English 7

Key point

Using pairs of commas

Commas are like scissors: they are used in pairs to show cuts in the sentence where words, phrases or clauses can be removed from the sentence without damaging the grammar. This means that when the words within the pair of commas are removed, there should still be a complete sentence left behind when what is left is joined up. For example, look at the following sentence: 'Rattlesnakes are, you must admit, something you wouldn't want in your house'. If you take out the words between the commas, you still have a sentence: 'Rattlesnakes are something you wouldn't want in your house'. This is a good test which you can use to check whether you are putting your commas around the right words in the sentence: if you take out those words, what is left still has to make sense.

5. A shape poem is one in which the layout of the words reflects an aspect of the subject of the poem. You are going to write a shape poem about a snake.

   a What comes into your mind when you think of snakes? Contribute to a brainstorm on the board of the connotations and associations of this creature.

   b Look back at Text 7A and collect some words or ideas for describing your snake, which can be any type of snake you wish. Think about your own experience with snakes.

   c Organise your ideas into a sequence and write them in the shape of a snake. Text 7B on the next page is an example, but your poem can make a different shape, such as a coil or a series of humps, as long as it represents the appearance and movement of a snake. Read out and then display your poem.

UNIT 7 Down to earth

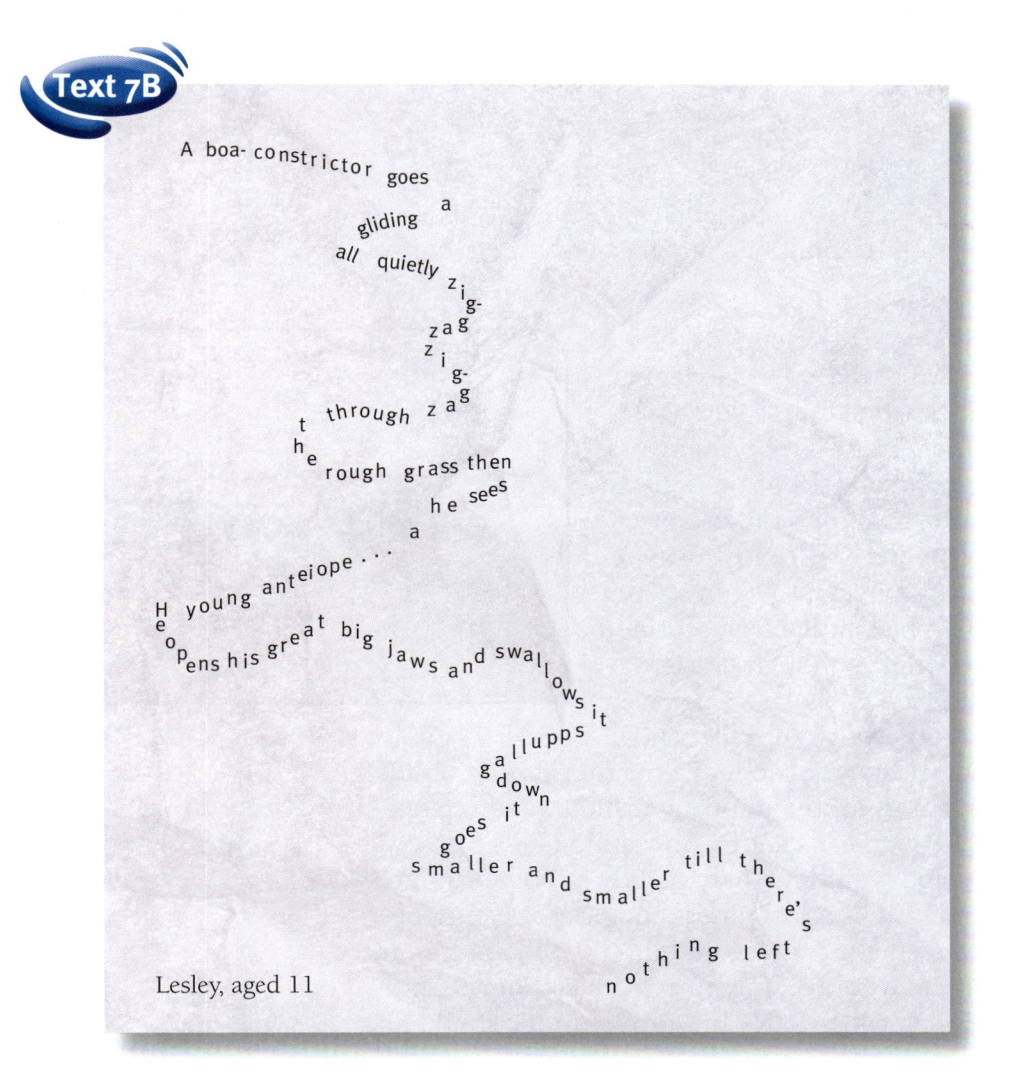

Text 7B

A boa-constrictor goes a gliding all quietly zig-zag zig-zag through the rough grass then he sees a young antelope... He opens his great big jaws and swallows it gallupps down goes it smaller and smaller till there's nothing left

Lesley, aged 11

6 a Read Text 7C on the next page. Using your own words, summarise in one sentence each:
  i how the boy found scorpions
  ii what happened when he did
  iii how he felt about scorpions.

b Find the words or phrases in the first paragraph which best describe the appearance of the scorpions. Some of these are similes or metaphors, because they make effective descriptions, as long as the comparisons are appropriate.

c The boy calls the scorpions *he*, and he talks to the reader as *you*. Can you comment on this use of personal pronouns? What do you think it adds to the account?

The world in a wall

Text 7C is a passage from *My Family and Other Animals* by Gerald Durrell. It gives a child's account of studying a creature in a garden on a Greek island.

The shyest and most self-effacing **of** the wall community were the most dangerous; you hardly ever saw one unless you looked **for** it, and yet there must have been several hundred living **in** the cracks **of** the wall. Slide a knife-blade carefully **under** a piece **of** loose plaster and lever it gently **away from** the brick, and there, crouching **beneath** it, would be a little black scorpion an inch long, looking <u>as</u> though he were made **out of** polished chocolate. They were weird-looking things, **with** their flattened, oval bodies, their neat, crooked legs, and enormous crab-like claws, bulbous and <u>as</u> neatly jointed <u>as</u> armour, and the tail <u>like</u> a string **of** brown beads ending **in** a sting <u>like</u> a rose-thorn. The scorpion would lie there quietly <u>as</u> you examined him, only raising his tail **in** an almost apologetic gesture **of** warning if you breathed too hard **on** him. If you kept him **in** the sun too long he would simply turn his back **on** you and walk away, and then slide slowly but firmly **under** another section **of** plaster.

   I grew very fond **of** these scorpions. I found them to be pleasant, unassuming creatures **with**, **on** the whole, the most charming habits. Provided you did nothing silly or clumsy (<u>like</u> putting your hand **on** one) the scorpions treated you **with** respect, their one desire being to get away and hide <u>as</u> quickly <u>as</u> possible. They must have found me rather a trial, for I was always ripping sections **of** the plaster away so that I could watch them, or capturing them and making them walk about **in** jam jars so that I could see the way their feet moved. By means **of** my sudden and unexpected assaults **on** the wall I discovered quite a bit **about** the scorpions.

UNIT 7 Down to earth

7 a Look at the use of the words *as* and *like* in Text 7C, which have been underlined. *As* and *like* are both used to make comparisons, but what is the difference in the way they are used? Here are some more examples:

She laughs as I do. = She laughs like me.

It walked like a crab. = It walked as a crab does.

Decide with a partner what you think the rule is.

b Now write three sentences of your own about scorpions, using *as* (or *as if* or *as though*) and *like*, to show that you have understood the grammatical difference (i.e. that *as* must be followed by a verb, but *like* is followed by a noun or pronoun).

8 The words in bold in Text 7C are prepositions. In this activity you will look at how they are used. First read the key point about prepositions on the next page to help you.

a Copy the table into your notebook and complete it with the prepositions from the passage in the correct column.

Prepositions which . . .		
show position	convey ideas	belong with a verb
on the table	in conclusion	make up

b Sometimes the choice of preposition changes the meaning of a phrase, e.g. 'in the beginning' (time) and 'at the beginning' (place). Copy the sentences below into your notebook and choose the possible prepositions that could go in the gaps. Explain the different meanings in each pair.

  i She didn't think she could finish the work ____ time.
   She didn't think she could finish the work ____ time.

  ii ____ the way, I don't like scorpions.
   ____ the way, I saw a scorpion.

  iii I didn't think much ____ her.
   I didn't think much ____ her.

  iv ____ the time they arrived, it was all over.
   ____ the time it didn't seem possible.

  v I have something ____ my mind at the moment.
   I have it ____ mind to do something about it.

c The prepositions *between* and *among* are often confused. Copy the sentences below into your notebook and choose the correct preposition to complete them.
  i The wall is ____ our garden and the neighbour's field.
  ii My mother told us to share the sweets ____ the three of us.
  iii ____ you and me, I don't believe he is telling the truth.
  iv The teacher told the students that they could talk ____ themselves until she returned.
  v There is not much difference ____ the alternative suggestions, but I think there should be a vote ____ the club members.

Key point

Prepositions

Prepositions are words that tell us the position of things, physically or as ideas, or words that follow or add to the meaning of certain verbs. Prepositions need to be followed by a noun or pronoun.
- They can specify where one thing is in relation to another, e.g. The scorpion is under the plaster.
- They can be part of a phrase which conveys an idea rather than in place e.g. on average, in conclusion, beyond all doubt.
- They can follow a verb which takes that preposition, e.g. interested in, look for. Verbs which have a similar meaning often take the same preposition, e.g. occupied *in*, engaged *in*, absorbed *in*; search *for*, hope *for*, long *for*.
- They can be a fixed part of a phrasal verb, one which has a special meaning because of the preposition(s) which follow it, e.g. look forward to, put up with.

Many prepositions have to be learnt because there is no obvious rule for their use, e.g. he got *out of* the car but he got *off* the bus; *on* foot but *by* bicycle. Sometimes, however, there is a rule, e.g. 'between' applies to two things or people, but 'among' must be used if there are more than two.

UNIT 7 Down to earth

Text 7D

This is the beginning of a poem about a tortoise.

Baby tortoise

You know what it is to be born alone,
Baby tortoise!

The first day to heave your feet little by little from the shell,
Not yet awake,
And remain lapsed on earth,
Not quite alive.

A tiny, fragile, half-animate bean.

To open your tiny beak-mouth, that looks as if it would never open,
Like some iron door;
To lift the upper hawk-beak from the lower base
And reach your skinny little neck
And take your first bite at some dim bit of herbage,
Alone, small insect,
Tiny bright-eye,
Slow one.

To take your first solitary bite
And move on your slow, solitary hunt.
Your bright, dark little eye,
Your eye of a dark disturbed night,
Under its slow lid, tiny baby tortoise,
So indomitable.

No one ever heard you complain.

D.H. Lawrence

9 Read the poem extract in Text 7D, noticing particularly the images.

a List the five different things the tortoise, or parts of the tortoise, are being compared to in the poem.

b Choose the comparison that you think is most effective and appropriate, and write a sentence explaining why.

c Can you think of an image of your own which compares a tortoise or part of a tortoise to something else? Write it down and share it with the class.

10 a Choose one of the photographs below and make notes of ways to describe the creature's movements, including images.

UNIT 7 Down to earth

b Now add some ideas for how you could describe its appearance, including images.

c Write a poem in free verse, in the style of Text 7D and about the same length, about your chosen creature. Address it in the same way as the tortoise is addressed, i.e. the second person as *you*.

Text 7E

Lost in the outback

In this extract from James Vance Marshall's novel *Walkabout*, two children, Mary and Peter, are alone in the outback, the vast expanse of uncultivated land in Australia.

At first the going was easy. Close to the stream, rocks of granite and quartz provided safe footing; and the trees, sprouting from every pocket of clay, were thick enough to give a welcome shade, but not so thick that they hindered progress. Mary pushed steadily on.

Soon the gully became wider, flatter, fanning into an open plain. Another tiny river joined theirs, and together the two of them went looping away down a shallow, sand-fringed valley. In the middle of the valley the undergrowth was thick; luxuriant. Brambles and underscrub slowed down their progress. But Mary didn't want to lose sight of the stream. Determinedly she forced a way through the tangle of vegetation, turning every now and then to give her brother a hand. Ground-vines coiled and snaked and clutched at their feet; the decaying trunks of fallen trees perversely blocked their path; but the girl kept on, sorting out a line of least resistance, holding back the lower branches to protect Peter from their swing back.

To start with – at least for the boy – it was an amusing game; part of their Big Adventure. They looked in the stream for fish; but the fish, such as they were, were asleep: invisible in the sediment-mud. They looked in the trees for birds; but the birds had vanished with the dawn. They looked in the bush for animals; but the animals were all asleep, avoiding the heat of the sun in carefully chosen burrow, log or cave. They looked among the riverside rocks for lizards; but the reptiles heard their clumsy approach, and slid soundlessly into crack or crevice. The bush slept: motionless: silent: apparently deserted. Drugged to immobility by the heat of the midday sun.

11 Listen to Text 7E being read out loud, and concentrate on the sounds of the words and the grammar structures. With a partner, find examples in Text 7E of:

   a alliteration (words close together which begin with the same sound)

   b assonance (words close together which repeat the same vowel sound)

   c personification, i.e. objects described as if they were human or animal (this can make them seem more threatening)

   d things described using triple structures, i.e. three adjectives, verbs or adverbs (this can emphasise their importance)

   e vocabulary or grammatical structures that are deliberately repeated (this can draw attention to the drama or seriousness of a situation).

12 Plan a piece of personal, reflective writing which gives an account of an experience you had outdoors, when you encountered something in your garden or near your home or in a park. Read the tip about making it feel real to help you. You can refer back to Texts 7A, 7C and 7E as possible models for the structure.

Tip

For Activity 12
Making it feel real

Text 7E comes from a work of fiction, but it sounds like informative writing because it is factual and descriptive. Your writing should use the first person and give the impression that the event really happened – even if it didn't – through the use of specific detail. It should contain some description of the setting and of whatever it was you saw, to make the location and creature imaginable to the reader. It should also include your thoughts about the encounter, both at the time and afterwards. Perhaps it changed your mind about whether you liked or disliked the creature.

   You can practise using stylistic effects and poetic devices too: triple adjectives; repeated grammar structures; alliteration; assonance; personification. Repetition is permissible when it is being used deliberately by the writer to create a particular effect.

UNIT 8 Hidden treasure

In this unit you will read about some famous adventure journeys so that you can compare them and practise writing this kind of story. You will look at the difference between active and passive verbs, and learn more about commas, relative clauses and the apostrophe of possession.

Activities

1 Quests, which are the basis for many games and much children's literature, are a popular form of fantasy which involves a journey through perils to reach the goal of finding something lost or precious. The tales are fast-moving, with a set structure and character types, and they use symbolic names, objects and numbers. They often also include prophecies, spells, dreams, maps and clues.

  a Think of stories (some may be films) where the characters set off in search of something, and say what it is they are searching for.

  b How do such stories usually begin, and how do they usually end?

  c What are the typical characters and events in such stories?

Key point

Adventure quest characters

- There are usually more male than female main characters.
- There is usually an old man, who is wise and who will guide the hero, or who is about to die and has a secret to pass on.
- The hero is typically an innocent and inexperienced young man who is chosen because of his bravery and trustworthiness to go on a quest for something to save the country from the threat of an evil monster or tyrant. He will grow up while away and return home wiser about the ways of the world.
- The hero takes a loyal friend with him, who is often a servant rather than an equal, and less intelligent but useful.

Cambridge Checkpoint English 7

- These three types of character (the old man, the hero, and the hero's loyal friend) remain on the side of good throughout the story, but they will be tested and will have to undergo fearful experiences and life-threatening dangers, such as fighting duels, in order to be victorious in the end.
- There will usually be two types of evil character: a powerful lord or witch and the underlings who carry out their commands or who have fallen under a spell.
- Finally, there are helpful characters met on the journey who appear briefly to give important information, warnings or aid to the hero.

Text 8A

Plot synopsis 1

This is the storyline of the magic adventure novel *The Lion, the Witch and the Wardrobe*, by C.S. Lewis, the first in a series of stories about the land of Narnia.

In 1940 four siblings – Peter, Susan, Edmund, and Lucy – <u>are evacuated</u> from London to escape the bomb attacks of World War II. They <u>are sent</u> to live with a Professor, who lives in a large house in the countryside. While the four children are exploring the house, Lucy looks into a wardrobe and discovers a **portal** to a magical world, which <u>is named</u> Narnia. The landscape <u>is covered</u> by snow, as it is under a spell of 'always winter and never Christmas'. There Lucy meets a **faun** named Tumnus, who invites her to tea in his home and tells her he she should be reported to the tyrannical White Witch, the Queen of Narnia, who captures humans.

When she returns to the real world, Lucy's siblings do not believe her story about Narnia, but her unpleasant elder brother, Edmund, follows her through the back of the wardrobe on her next trip and <u>is met</u> by the White Witch, who enchants him with sweets. She encourages him to bring his siblings to her in Narnia by promising that he can rule over them. Edmund returns home and lies to Peter and Susan, *spitefully* denying Lucy's claim about the existence of Narnia.

Eventually all four of the children enter Narnia together while hiding in the wardrobe. Lucy discovers Mr Tumnus has been imprisoned by the witch and asks her siblings to help her to find him. They meet Mr and Mrs Beaver, who invite them to dinner and recount a prophecy that the White Witch's power will fail when four children – two male and two female – fill the four thrones at Cair Paravel. The Beavers tell of the true king of Narnia – a great lion named Aslan – who after many years' absence is now 'on the move again'. Edmund **sneaks** away to see the White Witch, whose castle is filled with the stone statues of her former enemies.

The Beavers, realising where Edmund has gone, lead the other children to Aslan. As they travel, they notice that the snow is melting, indicating that the White Witch's spell is breaking. This is confirmed by Father Christmas, whom they **encounter** on the way. The children and the Beavers meet with Aslan and his army. Peter takes part in his first battle with a sword given to him by Father Christmas, killing a wolf who threatens Susan.

The Witch approaches to speak with Aslan, insisting that according to magic tradition she has the right to execute Edmund as a traitor because he has escaped from her power. Aslan speaks with her *privately* and persuades her not to put him to death. That evening, Aslan *secretly* leaves the camp but is followed by Lucy and Susan. They discover that Aslan has offered his own life in exchange for Edmund's. Aslan is tied to the Stone Table and then killed by the Witch with a knife. The following morning, however, Aslan is *miraculously* alive again, because someone who *willingly* dies in the place of another is allowed to return to life.

Aslan allows Lucy and Susan to ride on his back as he hurries to the Witch's castle. There he breathes upon the statues and they come alive. Peter and Edmund lead the Narnian army in a battle against the White Witch's army, but they are losing until Aslan arrives with the former statues as **reinforcements**. The Narnians defeat the evil army, and the Witch is killed by the victorious Aslan. The children are named kings and queens of Narnia.

Several years later, and now adult, the siblings go hunting for a White Stag. *Suddenly*, tree branches turn into coathangers, and they find themselves back in the wardrobe as children again.

> **faun** a mythical forest spirit, half human and half goat

2 a Does Text 8A remind you of any other stories that you know? What are the similarities?

  b How many different animals are referred to in the story? Why do you think it is common to use talking animals in fantasy and quest stories?

  c Copy the table below into your notebook and complete it, saying what kind of character you would expect the types of animal to be, judging from stories that you know, as well as Text 8A.

Animal	Character
wolf	
fox	
lion	
deer	
owl	
rabbit	
cat	
snake	

  d Entry into another world by a strange route is common to many adventure fantasy stories. List other examples you can think of.

  e Judging from stories that you know, as well as Text 8A, what do you think the following symbols represent in adventure quests?

3 In this activity you will look more closely at the vocabulary in Text 8A.

  a Find the following five words in Text 8A (they are in bold in the passage). Give synonyms for them which fit the context and are the same part of speech. You may need to use a thesaurus to help you. (Look at the key point on synonyms and vocabulary on page 130 in Unit 10 as well.)

  evacuated   portal   sneaks   encounter   reinforcements

  b Now find the adverbs in Text 8A, which are in italics. Work in pairs to decide what the rule is for why some end in *ly* and some end in *lly*. Look at the key point about adverb endings on the next page to help you.

UNIT 8 Hidden treasure

Key point

Adverb endings

Adverbs are formed from the adjective by adding *ly*, for example *mysterious* ➔ *mysteriously*. Those which appear to end in *lly* have *ly* added to an adjective which already ended in *l*, therefore making it double, for example *faithful* ➔ *faithfully*. There are some exceptions to this rule, such as *fast*, *hard* and *seldom*, which are adverbs although they do not end in *ly*. You also need to know that if the adjective ends in *ic*, as in *frantic*, *dramatic* and *specific*, for example, an *al* is usually added as well, so that the adverb form is *frantically*, *dramatically* and *specifically*. Note that adverbs never end in *ley*, though this is a common misspelling.

c   There are several negative prefixes in English. A prefix is a group of letters which can be put on the front of a word to add to or change its meaning. Copy the table below into your notebook and put the words in the correct column according to which negative prefix they take (some have more than one possible answer).

| allows | appropriate | belief | confirmed | cover |
| lead | pleasant | possible | rule | courage |

dis	in or im	mis	un

4 This activity focuses on aspects of grammar in Text 8A.

a   In addition to *who* and *which*, which you looked at in Unit 6, there are two other words which can be used to make relative clauses, as shown in the sentences below from Text 8A:

'This is confirmed by Father Christmas, <u>whom</u> they encounter on the way.'
'Edmund sneaks away to see the White Witch, <u>whose</u> castle is filled with the stone statues of her former enemies.'

Try to work out why these words are being used here instead of *who*. Then read the key point on the next page and write two sentences of your own, using *whose* in one and *whom* in the other, showing you have understood how they are used.

Key point

Relative clauses 2

You have seen that relative clauses can begin with *who* or *which* (see page 74 in Unit 6). They can also begin with *whom* or *whose*, as in the examples in Activity 4a. In the first example, *whom* refers to Father Christmas, but as Father Christmas is not the person performing the action of the verb (*encounter*) because it is the children who encounter him, we need the word *whom* not *who*. The form *whom* is also used following a preposition (e.g. 'to whom it may concern'). In the second example, *whose* = 'belonging to whom', and when it is put with 'castle' to give the phrase 'whose castle', it means 'the castle belonging to the White Witch'. *Whose* can refer to either people or things, because 'of which' doesn't have its own separate form, as in the example 'the house whose gate is broken'.

b For Activity 4b and 4c, first read the key point on active and passive verbs on page 101. Now look at the underlined verbs in Text 8A, which are passive (e.g. '. . . the Witch <u>is killed</u> by the victorious Aslan'). Copy and complete the following sentences with the passive form of the verb. Remember that to form the passive you use the verb *be* in the appropriate part and tense, followed by the past participle of the main verb (e.g. 'He was wanted urgently', where *was* is the past tense of the verb *be*, and *wanted* is the past participle of *want*).
  i When she returned, Lucy's story about Narnia _____ (not believe).
  ii Edmund _____ (encourage) to bring his siblings to Narnia.
  iii The four thrones must _____ (fill) by two girls and two boys.
  iv The other children _____ (lead) by the Beavers to Aslan.
  v The White Stag _____ (hunt) by the children when they found themselves back in the real world.

c Write the following sentences in your notebook, changing the passive verbs to the active form. For example, for 'The evil army is defeated by the Narnians', you would write 'The Narnians defeat the evil army'. You may have to make other small grammatical changes.
  i The country is named Narnia.
  ii Lucy is met by Mr Tumnus.
  iii They were invited to dinner by the Beavers.
  iv The two girls were allowed to ride on Aslan's back.
  v The statues were brought back to life by Aslan's breath.

UNIT 8 Hidden treasure

Key point

Active and passive verbs

The active form of the verb specifies or emphasises who is performing the action (e.g. 'The children escaped'). It is also a shorter form because the passive form requires one more verb part, so is less concise. However, it is sometimes necessary to use the passive. We use the passive when:
- the performer of the action is unknown
- it is not important to know who the performer is
- a more formal and official style is required (e.g. 'The winner will be declared').

We can still use the passive when the performer is known and we want to say who it is. We do this using the preposition *by* to introduce the performer of the action (e.g. 'They were taken there by Aslan').

Text 8B

Plot synopsis 2

Quest stories often involve travel by sea as well as overland. This is the storyline of an adventure novel called *Treasure Island*. Note that the commas have been removed from the first three paragraphs.

Jim Hawkins lives with his mother in an inn the Admiral Benbow on the south coast of England in a village called Black Hill Cove.

One day an ancient sailor Captain Billy Bones turns up there apparently intending to stay. He hires Jim to keep a look out for other sailors but despite all precautions he is hunted down by Blind Pew and Black Dog and served with the 'black spot' a symbol that means death.

A group of pirates raid the inn in search of the chest containing the old **sailor's** papers but they do not find them and Jim does. They include a map showing the location of the pirate **Flint's** buried treasure on Skeleton Island in the West Indies which

Jim Doctor Livesey and Squire Trelawney decide to go in search of. After finding a ship the 'Hispaniola' and a crew they set out on their voyage with Jim as the **ship's** cabin boy.

Unfortunately, the crew includes a one-legged pirate, Long John Silver, who also wants to find the treasure. He has a talking parrot, which sits on his shoulder. Jim, hidden in an apple barrel, overhears the **crew's** plan to *mutiny*, and he warns his *comrades* of the **pirates'** *conspiracy*.

The battle between the pirates and **Jim's** party is an exciting and bloody one, taking place both on the ship and on the *desert* island after they arrive. Jim discovers on the island a *marooned* sailor, Ben Gunn, left behind three years earlier, who shows him where Flint's treasure was buried and the cave in which he has now hidden it.

Jim manages to take control of the 'Hispaniola', but he is captured by Long John Silver on land. They do a deal that **Jim's** life will be spared in return for Long John Silver not being hanged for piracy when they return home.

In a few **weeks'** time, he disappears at the first port they stop at in America, with some of the gold guineas now in the **ship's** hold. Everyone else returns safe and rich to England.

5 a Give synonyms for the following words, in italics in Text 8B, as used in the context of the passage.

mutiny   comrades   conspiracy   desert   marooned

b What can you say about the names of people and places used in the passage? List them and say what associations each of them bring to mind.

c What would be a surprising ending to the story? Write a different final sentence which goes against the expectations for this kind of story.

6 You can see in the first three paragraphs of Text 8B how difficult it is for the reader to understand text without commas. For this activity you need a copy of Text 8B.

a On your copy of the text, put in the missing commas in the first three paragraphs. Remember that commas are used:
  i to separate clauses
  ii to separate items in a list
  iii to show words and phrases which are grammatically unnecessary and could be removed.

UNIT 8 Hidden treasure

b Look again at the last sentence in paragraph 2:

'Jim discovers on the island a marooned sailor, Ben Gunn, left behind three years earlier, who shows him where Flint's treasure was buried and the cave in which he has now hidden it.'

This is a complex sentence, with several clauses linked together and commas to separate them. If the information had been given in simple sentences (i.e. with one verb), it would have needed six sentences. Split the complex sentence into the six simple sentences, giving all the information, and write them in your notebook.

c On your copy of the text, find and circle all the apostrophes. What is their purpose in each case? Look at the key point on apostrophes to help you.

Key point

Apostrophe of possession

We usually show that something belongs to something or someone by putting an apostrophe and an *s* at the end of the owner. If the owner is singular, we put the apostrophe before the *s* (e.g. *Jim's mother*); if it is plural, we put the apostrophe after the *s* (e.g. *the pirates' plan*). If the noun forms an irregular plural (e.g. *children*, *people*, *men*), then the apostrophe goes before the *s* because the plural has already been formed in the word itself. If there is already an *s* at the end of the word denoting the owner, as in proper names like Claudius, then it is optional whether another *s* is added. (Some people feel a double 's' sound is very clumsy so they prefer to add only the apostrophe to show possession.) Whether a second *s* is added or not, the apostrophe always goes after the name and not in it. To show that Claudius possesses gold, for example, we put *Claudius's gold* or *Claudius' gold*. Remember that *his*, *hers*, *its*, *ours*, *yours* and *theirs* do not have an apostrophe. Note that time phrases can require an apostrophe, as in 'ten days' time'; which means 'ten days of time'.

7 Compare Text 8B with Text 8A. What are the similarities of:

a the types of character?

b the beginning and ending?

c the events which occur?

8 **a** In small groups, study the treasure map carefully, noticing the features which it illustrates. Give them names, e.g. Palm Beach.

b Decide where you think would be the best place to bury treasure, and put a cross to mark the spot.

c Write a set of instructions to explain to someone how to find the treasure using the map. Look back at the key point on giving directions on page 2 in Unit 1. You will have to tell them how far to go, in which direction, and how they will know they have arrived at the right place.

9 In small groups, create a scenario (sequence of events) to explain the existence of the treasure map in Activity 8. Imagine that a group of friends hid the treasure there.

a Decide on the answers to the following questions:
- What does the treasure consist of?
- Why was it buried?
- When was it buried?
- How was it buried?
- Who is the map for?

UNIT 8 Hidden treasure

b Give yourselves character names, and draft the script of a scene of a play in which the friends discuss and decide where to bury the treasure, and the reasons for and difficulties of doing so. Read the key point about writing playscripts to help you.

c Practise and then perform your play to the rest of the class.

Key point

Writing playscripts

When you write a script, you can put the names of the speakers in the margin to show who is speaking, and you don't have to use speech marks. Try to balance out the speeches so that everyone gets a turn and roughly the same amount to say. You can put in stage directions in square brackets to indicate any significant movements or facial expressions which the speaker should perform, for example [She points in the direction of the ship]; [with a sinister smile]. Contractions such as *can't* instead of *cannot* can be used as this is oral and informal speech. Sometimes one character interrupts another and does not let them finish what they were going to say, which conveys excitement, impatience or another strong emotion. The characters should not agree with each other, at least at first, but have conflicting opinions, as this is what creates tension and drama.

Text 8C

The Knight's riddle

This is the beginning of a story which sets a test, which is a type of quest.

One winter's day the King was hunting in the forest with his men when a white deer stepped into view. 'Keep still, everyone,' said the King, 'I intend to kill this deer myself.' Holding his bow in one hand and his arrows over his shoulder, the King crept up on the deer until, deep in the heart of the forest, he slew the deer with one shot. As the animal fell, a tall figure stepped from the shadows.

'How fortunate for me that we meet this way, with your arrow released from your hand so it cannot harm me,' boomed the voice of a strong and mighty Knight. 'For many years you have slandered my name and done me wrong . Now it is time for me to get my revenge.'

Thinking quickly, the King said, 'To slay me here, since you are armed and I dressed humbly in my hunting clothes, would bring you no honour, and shame would follow you for the rest of your life. I'll grant you anything you care to name – any amount of land or gold – to spare my life.'

'There is no land or gold, of any amount, that I desire,' said the Knight. 'However, I will get what I seek in an honourable way. I'll give you a chance to solve a riddle. One year and a day from now, you must appear before me here in these woods, without companions and without weapons. If at that time you are unable to solve this riddle, there can be no objection to my taking your life. But if you answer the riddle correctly, there will be no battle and you will be free to leave. You must swear on your honour that you will return in one year and a day, as I have commanded.'

'I agree to your terms,' said the King. 'What is the riddle?'

UNIT 8 Hidden treasure

10 a Draft a continuation of this story, of about one page. It does not have to complete the story. Bear in mind the following points.
- The characters need to speak and behave in the ways which have already been established.
- The plot and setting which have been provided need to be sustained and developed.
- The style, which is old-fashioned, needs to be similar enough to sound like a continuation by the same writer. Use the tip below to help you.

> **Tip**
>
> **For Activity 10**
> **Writing in an old-fashioned style**
>
> Writing in an old-fashioned style means choosing archaic vocabulary, i.e. words you know but which are no longer in everyday use, such as *slay* for *kill*, *oath* for *promise*, or *grant* for *allow*. This is the language of fairy tales and legends, which are usually set in medieval times and which use the same kind of characters, settings, events and objects, such as knights, forests, battles, arrows and gold.

11 You are going to write an outline for a quest story of your own, using some of the ideas you have collected during your study of this unit. You can refer back to your answers to Activity 9 to help you, and to Texts 8B and 8C as models. Use the following checklist to make sure you have covered everything.
- Does your story have a title?
- Does the country have a name?
- Have you described the appearance and qualities of your hero(es), and given them names?
- Does at least one of the good characters have a magic property or symbolic object to carry?
- Have you created an evil enemy, described their appearance and special powers, and given them a name?
- Is the objective of the quest clear? What is it called? What can it do? Where is it hidden?
- Is there a spell, prophecy or promise referred to in the story?
- Is there a character who is met on the journey and who helps the hero?
- Does a decisive contest or battle occur?
- Have you said how the hero gets home?

12
a Plan your quest short story. Consider the following questions in the planning stage.
   i   Which characters do you need to introduce immediately?
   ii How can you use dialogue to establish character?
   iii How will you convey economically the necessary plot information?
   iv How will you create the setting, the time and the place?
   v   Which of the four types of narrative opening you have looked at so far (character, setting, dialogue, action) would be the most suitable for this type of story? Look back at the key point on beginning stories on page 77 in Unit 6.

b Draft your short story, of about two sides of writing. Pay attention to the layout and punctuation of dialogue, and think about where to start a new paragraph.

c Write a final copy of your story. You could write it by hand or on a computer.

UNIT 9 Meet the family

This unit focuses on descriptions and views of family members and family life, including pets. You will look at more vocabulary, spelling, punctuation and conditional sentences, and there will be further practice in writing dialogue and doing selective summaries. You will also look at the role of rhythm and tone in poetry.

Activities

1. **a** A dictionary definition of the word *family* is 'A household, all those who live in one house; parents and children'. Write your own definition.

    b Draw a family tree of your immediate family showing three generations: your grandparents, your parents and their siblings, and your siblings and cousins.

    c Explain your family tree to a partner.

A day in the life of the goddess Taleju

This is an account of a day in the life of an unusual 15-year-old girl called Chanira, who is worshipped as a goddess in Nepal.

I wake around 6, but my duties as a *kumari* – a living incarnation of the Hindu goddess Taleju – don't start until later. I wear red robes to bed, but I change into more elaborate ones with gold embroidery for daytime and I put on my jewellery. My father always does my make-up for me. He is an artist and my mother is a housewife, and I have two younger brothers, aged 13 and 10. I live with my family in Lalitpur in Kathmandu. I have been a *kumari* for as long as I can remember.

At 8 we do *puja*, a religious ritual that must be performed every day. I sit on my throne in my *puja* room and my mother will bring offerings of fruit and rice on special metal platters. She burns incense, lights butter lamps and recites mantras. When I am in the puja room I am the goddess Taleju. Nobody is allowed to speak to me and I must not talk. Perhaps it's because of this that even outside the puja room I am very uncomfortable speaking to people, apart from my family.

Puja usually takes half an hour, and after that I have my breakfast of *chiya* and *roti*. Then I do my homework. I have been working hard this year because I had to take my school leaving exam in the spring. Now I'm doing my equivalent to A-levels.

UNIT 9 Meet the family

After my homework we sit down to our main meal, which we have before midday. It's always dahl, curry and rice. At 12 I go back to the puja room, and between then and 1 p.m. I receive devotees. I bless them with a *tikka* (a spot of red dust) on the forehead. They bring fruit, rice or coconut, bow down before me and say 'Namaste'. People might think it feels odd to sit on a throne and give blessings, but it doesn't to me because it's what I have always done. I was six when I became a *kumari*. My mother says she knew from the moment I was born that I was unique. She says I looked very knowing.

The priests decide who becomes a *kumari*, and make the choice based on a girl's age, horoscope and physical attributes.

At 1 p.m. my lessons start. I have three teachers who come to the house. My brothers go to the local school, but I am not allowed to leave the house, except on one of the 19 annual festival days. Then, as Taleju, I am carried through the streets in a **palanquin** to be present at all the ceremonies. I cannot talk to anyone; I can only watch the rites in the temple.

I never think about going outside. I think if I were to sneak out to buy sweets or anything like that, I should feel sick – it's not how a *kumari* behaves. If I did something a goddess should not do, who knows what impact it could have on the Nepali people?

When another local girl takes over from me as *kumari*, I'd like to go on to college and study accountancy. I believe that if you study hard, you can do anything in life.

My lessons finish at 7, and at 8 we have our evening meal, which is the same as the morning's. I am allowed to eat with my family, but my food has to be prepared separately, in special dishes that have to be ritually cleaned.

In the evening I watch television or go on the computer – I have a Hotmail account – and hang out with my brothers. So I suppose that for an hour or so I'm a normal teenager. But because of my duties I have always been too busy to play, so I don't have any of my own friends.

I can't really begin to imagine what my life will be like when I am able to go outside with my brothers and to college. Right now I am just living from day to day, and because I'm always with my family, whom I love, I enjoy that. I go to bed at 10, in my own room, which has a small wooden bed. I never dream.

palanquin a covered chair carried on poles on the shoulders of four bearers

2 Read Text 9A. In this activity you will have a closer look at some of the vocabulary in the article, and at spelling.

a The words on the left are from the article. Write them in your notebook alongside the correct synonym from the list of words on the right. You may need to use a dictionary to help you.

incarnation	prediction
elaborate	influence
ritual	unequalled
unique	decorated
horoscope	performance
attributes	representative
impact	qualities

b The following words from the article are considered difficult to spell. Underline the hot spot (difficult part) of each and focus on it long enough to memorise it. Then write out the words without looking at them. Check back to see if you've spelt them correctly.

jewellery	unique
special	physical
uncomfortable	college
equivalent	separately
receive	ceremonies

c The word *receive* is an example of the spelling rule:

i before *e*,
except after *c*,
when the sound you are making
is double *ee*.

Give three examples of words with *ie* spelling, and three with *ei* spelling following a *c*.

3 **a** Imagine you are Chanira's mother. Describe your daughter in your own words but using information from Text 9A to show how you see her.

b Imagine you are Chanira's 13-year-old brother. Describe your sister in your own words but using information from Text 9A to show what you think of her.

c In one paragraph, summarise what Chanira does each day.

UNIT 9 Meet the family

Key point

Selective summary

A selective summary means that you must identify and use only the parts of a text which are relevant to the question and you must ignore the rest. It's a good idea to underline the question so that when you are highlighting the relevant parts of the text you can stay focused on it. This is especially necessary when the question has more than one part to it.

When you have found all the information which needs to be included in your summary, you should transfer the ideas from it – in your own words as far as possible – into a plan. Use the plan to decide how to group and order the points in your summary, and indicate this by using arrows, brackets and numbers. Write your summary in compound sentences using *and*, *but*, *so* and *or*, or complex sentences, e.g. those containing *who* or *which* (or *whose* or *whom*) or present participles. Look back at the key points on relative clauses on page 74 in Unit 6 and page 100 in Unit 8 to remind you.

4 **a** Reread Text 9A, making a list as you do so of the topics included in the description of daily life, such as what is eaten at mealtimes.

b Now make notes of the information you will give on these topics about yourself and your family.

c Draft an account of a typical day in your life, of about one page of writing. Use a chronological order, starting with getting up and finishing with going to bed. Use the tip below to help you.

Tip

For Activity 4c
Using a variety of sentences

This piece is a written monologue. It can sound monotonous if all the sentences begin with *I* so aim to begin each sentence differently. Because it is informative writing, and therefore clarity is important, the sentences can be simple (one verb), or compound (two or more verbs joined with *and*, *but*, *so* or *or*). Some relative clauses can be used for variety and fluency. You will notice that in Text 9A there are some sentences beginning with *But*. This is not normally encouraged. Here it shows that it is a child speaking, and that features of spoken English are being used because it is trying to sound like an oral text.

Family talk

The first cry of a newborn baby in Chicago or Zamboango, in Amsterdam or Rangoon, has the same pitch and key, each saying, 'I am! I have come through! I belong! I am a member of the Family!'

Carl Sandburg

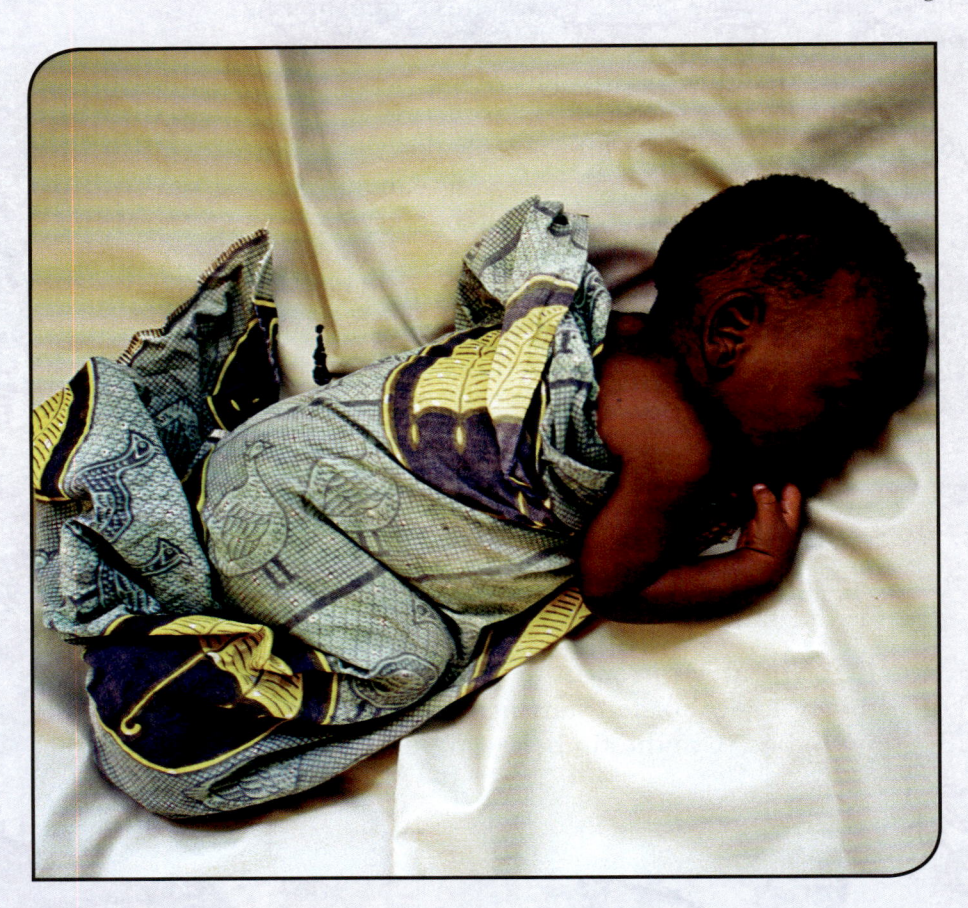

The morning my sister was born, my Dad slipped a note under my pillow while I was still asleep. It said: 'Congratulations! You've got a baby sister.' I woke, found it, grunted, shoved the note back under my pillow and went to sleep again.

When I saw her for the first time I was surprised. I'd expected her either to have a head of hair, or none at all. What I saw was a thin strip of jet-black hair that ran like a mane down the centre of her head. On balance, I decided she was quite interesting and that having a sister would be all right.

UNIT 9 Meet the family

> I was seven when my sister was born and I'd never had to share things with another child. Not that I remember it as a problem. Previously, I'd invented half a million games-to-play-by-yourself; now I had someone to talk to, read to, play with – teach to walk. Later we fell out – partly because she was too clever. I'd teach her card games, for instance, then she'd beat me. We had arguments. I threatened to hit her. She threatened to tell Mum or Dad. I hit her. She told Mum or Dad. Sometimes they hit *me*. There were variations on this theme but I always seemed to find myself on the losing end!
>
> From *Family Talk* by Rex Harley

5 You need a copy of Text 9B for this activity. Look for and circle the following punctuation marks on your copy of the passage. Discuss with a partner how each is being used. Tell the class what you have decided about the rules.

  a Exclamation marks (!). Note that they are used singly.

  b Hyphens (-). Note that there is no space between the letters and the hyphen.

  c Dashes (–). Note that they are double the length of a hyphen and that there is a space either side of them.

6 **a** Think of an occasion like the one in Text 9B. Do you remember the birth of a younger sibling or another addition to the family? Reflect on your relationship with your siblings (or your cousins, if you don't have any siblings) and how you played together, and what you thought of them.

  b Decide what you want to say about your brother, sister or cousin. Make some notes of what you are going to write.

  c Write a personal reflection about your chosen relative, about the same length as Text 9B. You should practise using hyphens, dashes and exclamation marks appropriately.

Text 9C

An unusual family pet
- Skunks are members of the weasel family.
- The species is native to the Americas, Indonesia and the Philippines.
- They have soft black fur with a distinctive white stripe.
- They live an average of 10 years, but sometimes up to 20.
- They vary in length from 20 cm to 40 cm and weigh up to 8 kg.
- They spray a strong malodorous liquid when they feel threatened.
- It is illegal to remove their scent glands.
- They are naturally nocturnal.
- They bite, but can be trained to stop.
- They can be house-trained and will use a litter tray.
- They are increasingly popular and fashionable as pets.
- They can cost about £2000 or $2500 in a shop.
- They are affectionate and sociable, and will sleep cuddled up with humans or dogs.
- They can be taken for a walk on a lead.
- They are omnivores and eat small rodents, as well as fruit and nuts.
- They will eat dog food.

7 a Copy the table below into your notebook and complete it with the relevant facts about skunks, separating the facts **for** from the facts **against** keeping a skunk as a household pet. Not all the facts should be used, and some could be used in both columns.

Keeping a skunk as a pet	
For	Against

UNIT 9 Meet the family

b Write a short speech to a parent, of about half a page, using the relevant information from the 'for' column, in which you try to persuade them to let you have a pet skunk to live in the house.

c Write your parent's reply, of about the same length, giving the reasons why they do not agree to your request. The speeches can be performed to the class as a dialogue.

Text 9D

Baby hippo becomes a one-ton daughter

That morning in March 2000, 63-year-old Tonie Joubert saw a newborn baby hippo washed up onto the lawn of his riverside home near Hoedspruit in South Africa. The River Blyde had flooded and almost reached his house.

Joubert found that the baby hippo was only a few hours old. 'She was very, very weak, so weak she couldn't stand up. I knew I had to save her life', says Joubert, a game ranger. He nursed and bottle-fed the 15 kilo baby back to health with the help of his wife, Shirley.

She survived, and grew, and grew. She became a giant – and she also became convinced that she was part of the family. She now weighs nearly three-quarters of a ton. Like most teenagers, she finds family life too comfortable to want to leave home, and has a double life which includes wild hippos as well as the family. Attempts to reintroduce her to the wild have all failed. And, being free to roam, the danger now is that she will be attacked and killed by other hippos – or shot by local farmers protecting their animals and crops.

Jessica eats, sleep, swims and plays with Tonie and Shirley. What's more, she wanders round the house, drinks coffee on the verandah, hangs out with the family dogs, and enjoys Shirley's soothing massages that help her relax at the end of a happy hippo day. She greets Tonie with special grunts and flicking ears whenever she sees him, and follows him like a dog wherever he goes. She has shown problem-solving abilities and a willingness to respond to commands. When Joubert says the Afrikaans word for yes, she closes her eyes; when he tells her to sit, she sits. She has never shown any aggression.

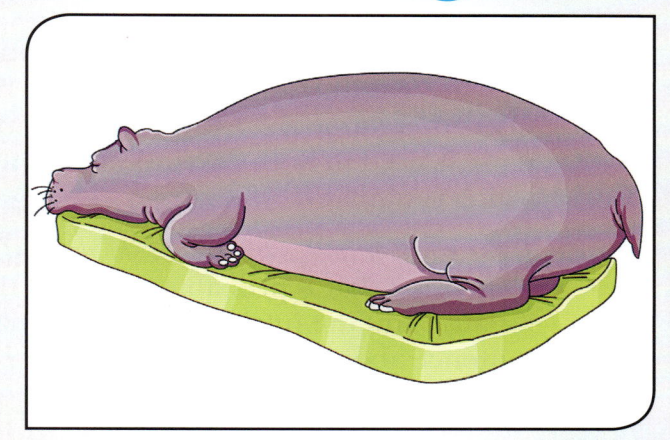

The daily routine includes 10 litres of sweet warm coffee fed through a bottle, and dog biscuits as special treats. Although she returns to the river most evenings for a mud bath, she also enjoys lying on the couple's bed. She not only covers it in slime, but has broken it three times. She has learned how to open doors by turning the key, so it's impossible to keep her out of the bedroom.

Her friend and potential mate, Charlie, was shot by a neighbouring farmer. 'Jessica is too trusting of humans,' says Shirley. 'Our constant fear now is that the same fate as Charlie's may befall our precious Jess, the gentlest creature on Earth.' But the couple are certain that if they had not rescued her she would have been eaten by a crocodile. And they and she would have missed out on joy and companionship.

The Jouberts aim to establish a hippo reserve where Jessica and the rest of the herd can live safely. 'These are beautiful creatures and we should look after them,' says Joubert.

Cambridge Checkpoint English 7

> **Key point**
>
> **Conditional sentences**
>
> There are four kinds of conditional sentences. A conditional clause begins with *If* (or *Unless* as the negative form) and is separated from the main clause by a comma. The *if*-clause can be either first or second in the sentence. The further back in the past the verb tense is, the less likely the condition is to be fulfilled and the event to happen.

8
a *If she hears a command, she obeys it.* This sentence is permanently true (i.e. there is the same response every time something happens – she obeys every time she hears a command), and the present simple tense is used in both parts. Write another sentence about Jessica which is similar.

b *If she trusts humans too much, she will suffer.* This sentence describes something that is probable, and uses the present simple in the *if*-clause and the future tense in the main clause. Write another sentence about Jessica which is similar.

c *If the couple established a hippo reserve, Jessica would be safe.* This sentence describes something that is possible, and uses the past simple in the *if*-clause and *would* plus the infinite part of the verb in the main clause. Write another sentence about Jessica which is similar.

d *If they had left Jessica in the river, she would have died.* This sentence describes something that is impossible, and uses the past perfect in the *if*-clause and *would* plus *have* plus the past participle of the verb in the main clause. Write another sentence about Jessica which is similar.

e Write four sentences beginning with *Unless* which use each of the types of conditional forms.

9 Make lists under three headings of the facts in Text 9D about the following topics:

a how the Jouberts came to adopt Jessica

b Jessica

c hippopotami.

UNIT 9 Meet the family

10 Write a news bulletin using the information collected in Activity 9. Begin the bulletin with the words: 'A couple in Hoedspruit, South Africa, have adopted a most unusual pet . . .' and use the information in the tip below to help you.

Tip

For Activity 10
News bulletins

A radio or TV news bulletin has to be brief but informative and is therefore filled with facts and names. To do this economically it puts several adjectives in front of each noun, as in '63-year-old game ranger Tonie Joubert'. If it is an amusing or upbeat story, as this is, it will try to end on a humorous or cheerful note. This can be achieved by using a quotation from one of the people involved or a reference to something amusing that the hippo does.

Text 9E

Presents from my aunts in Pakistan

They sent me a salwar kameez
        peacock-blue,
                and another
    glistening like an orange split open,
embossed slippers, gold and black
        points curling.
    Candy-striped glass bangles
        snapped, drew blood.
    Like at school, fashions changed
        in Pakistan –
the salwar bottoms were broad and stiff,
        then narrow.
My aunts chose an apple-green sari,
    silver-bordered
            for my teens.

I tried each satin-silken top –
        was alien in the sitting-room.
I could never be as lovely
        as those clothes –

        I longed
for denim and corduroy.
        My costume clung to me
            and I was aflame,
I couldn't rise up out of its fire,
    half-English,
        unlike Aunt Jamila.

I wanted my parents' camel-skin lamp –
    switching it on in my bedroom,
to consider the cruelty
        and the transformation
from camel to shade,
    marvel at the colours
        like stained glass.

My mother cherished her jewellery –
    Indian gold, dangling, filigree,
        But it was stolen from our car.
The presents were radiant in my wardrobe.
    My aunts requested cardigans
        from Marks and Spencers.

My salwar kameez
    didn't impress the schoolfriend
who sat on my bed, asked to see
    my weekend clothes.
But often I admired the mirror-work,
    tried to glimpse myself
        in the miniature
glass circles, recall the story
    how the three of us
        sailed to England.
Prickly heat had me screaming on the way.
    I ended up in a cot
in my English grandmother's dining-room,
    found myself alone,
        playing with a tin-boat.
I pictured my birthplace
    from fifties' photographs.
        When I was older
there was conflict, a fractured land
    throbbing through newsprint.

UNIT 9 Meet the family

> Sometimes I saw Lahore –
>   my aunts in shaded rooms,
> screened from male visitors,
>   sorting presents,
>   wrapping them in tissue.
>
> Or there were beggars, sweeper-girls
>   and I was there –
>   of no fixed nationality,
> staring through fretwork
>   at the Shalimar Gardens.
>
>   *Moniza Alvi*

11 **a** Text 9E is a poem written in prose (i.e. non-poetry) sentences, without capitals at the beginning of the lines unless they begin a new sentence. It also has an unusual layout. Discuss as a class what the reasons for this poetic form might be, and how it relates to the poem's content and message.

b What is the poem saying about clothes? Write a sentence to summarise the role played in our lives and relationships by items of clothing, according to the poem.

c What is the poem saying about identity? Write a sentence to summarise the problems of forming an idea of where one belongs, according to the poem.

Key point

Punctuation in poetry

Punctuation is important in poetry as well as prose; it determines whether or not you should stop at the end of a line, or run on into the next one to complete the meaning. It can also be used to create a mid-line pause to show balance or contrast, or, as in Text 9E a sense of breakdown and distance as signified by the dashes. Punctuation links with other devices which affect the rhythm of the poem. Remember that poems are written to be spoken aloud, not just read on the page. It is usual for lines of poetry to begin with a capital letter, regardless of the punctuation in the previous line. If a poem breaks this rule – and some modern poetry does – you need to notice it and ask yourself what effect the poet wanted to create by being unconventional.

Cambridge Checkpoint English 7

12 An inference is a view based on the available evidence in the passage. (See the key point on page 127 in Unit 10 for more information about making inferences from a text.)

a Infer how the persona (the speaker) feels about having left Pakistan, and about life in England.

b Infer how the mother feels about the sisters she left behind in Pakistan, and about her daughter.

c Now write about a page of a dialogue between the teenager and her mother, discussing their feelings about the move to England, and how they view the aunts still in Lahore. You can set it out as a drama script with the names in the margin. Begin your script:

Mother: Are you pleased with your presents from your aunties?

Moniza: . . .

Text 9F

My grandmother

She kept an antique shop – or it kept her.
Among Apostle spoons and Bristol glass,
The faded silks, the heavy furniture,
She watched her own reflection in the brass
Salvers and silver bowls, as if to prove
Polish was all, there was no need of love.

And I remember how I once refused
To go out with her, since I was afraid.
It was perhaps a wish not to be used
Like antique objects. Though she never said
That she was hurt, I still could feel the guilt
Of that refusal, guessing how she felt.

Later, too frail to keep a shop, she put
All her best things in one narrow room.
The place smelt old, of things too long kept shut,
The smell of absences where shadows come
That can't be polished. There was nothing then
To give her own reflection back again.

UNIT 9 Meet the family

> And when she died I felt no grief at all,
> Only the guilt of what I once refused.
> I walked into her room among the tall
> Sideboards and cupboards – things she never used
> But needed; and no finger marks were there,
> Only the new dust falling through the air.
>
> *Elizabeth Jennings*

13 Select and quote words and phrases from the poem to include as support in your answers to the following questions. Sometimes the same quotation can be used to show more than one thing. For example, 'things she never used/But needed' is a comment on two different aspects of the grandmother's attitude to objects. To help you, look back at the key point on the use of quotation on page 76 in Unit 6, and use the key point below.

   a What is the persona saying about her grandmother's life?

   b What is the persona saying about herself?

   c What is the persona saying about the relationship between herself and her grandmother?

14 Read the poem again in your head, concentrating on the sounds of the words, and the persona's voice.

   a Think about the rhythm of the poem. How would you describe it? Did you read the poem quickly or slowly, and why?

   b Is there a regular rhyme scheme, or any rhyme at all? Are the lines end-stopped or run-on?

   c Tone is the emotion you put into your voice to read a passage or poem. What kind of emotion do you think would be appropriate for this poem, and why, bearing in mind what you have said about the rhythm, rhyme and line endings?

Key point

Poetic form

The poem in Text 9F has a regular (fixed pattern) rhyme and metre, while the poem in Text 9E is in free verse, which means it has no regular rhyme scheme or metre and the lines are of different lengths. In poetry, the form and layout should match the subject and the feeling of the poem. So, for example, long lines or run-on lines represent something which takes a long time or cannot be contained, and short, end-stopped lines (with punctuation) suggest something completed or controlled.

15 Write your own poem about a grandparent or elderly relative.

  a Collect ideas, some of which may come from the texts and discussions in this unit. First decide what setting and atmosphere you wish your poem to have. Is it going to be a happy or sad poem? Use the tip below to help you.

  b Think about style as well as content: grammar, vocabulary and imagery all affect mood and atmosphere, and these affect tone.

  c Think about form and layout: verse breaks, line length, punctuation, run-on or end-stopped lines all affect pace and rhythm, and these affect tone. Look back at the key points in this unit about punctuation in poetry, page 121, and poetic form, above.

  d Decide on a title, draft your poem, read it to a partner and then try to make improvements.

  e Read your final version to the class. Put appropriate emotion into your voice. Look at the tip again for advice on reading your poem aloud.

> **Tip**
>
> **For Activity 15**
> **Creating mood and atmosphere in your poem**
>
> The mood of a poem is mostly determined by the setting which you place it in (e.g. an antique shop has connotations of the loss of the past), which should match how the persona is feeling. The atmosphere may then be either cheerful or subdued. The title will give a clue to this. The pace, fast or slow, and the rhythm (relaxed and flowing or tense and 'jerky') will depend on the kind of grammar and vocabulary (complex or simple, long or short words), and on how many punctuation marks and end-stops the lines have. When you read a poem aloud, you should observe the punctuation, and on use your voice to convey the mood of the poem and the feeling of the persona by adopting the appropriate intonation to show the relevant emotion.

UNIT 10 Mysteries and puzzles

This unit will show you how mystery is used and how suspense is built up in stories. Readers need to use close reading and inference to be able to fully understand clues and to make predictions. You will be introduced to more types of narrative opening and revisit viewpoint, and you will look at ballads, a narrative verse form. There will also be some pronunciation and vocabulary practice.

Activities

1
  a In what ways is the act of reading narrative like solving a mystery?

  b Which types of writing keep the reader involved in trying to solve a puzzle?

  c Which are your favourite kinds of story? Do they rely on creating mystery or setting puzzles?

Text 10A

Guess what happened

'If anyone has forgotten anything,' said Dorothy, as their heavily laden car drew away from the house and headed for the motorway, 'say so now, or for ever hold your peace.'

'Will we be in time for the ferry?' asked Susan, the youngest of the three children on the back seat.

'We shall if we don't have to go back to turn off the bathroom tap,' said her mother.

Last year it had been the bathroom tap. The year before that, someone had broken a window just as they were leaving. And the year they went camping, they left a dozen tins of cat food behind for Ollie, but took the tin-opener away with them, to the considerable inconvenience of the neighbours who came in to feed their pet. Holiday departures were always occasions of stress and error. 'But this year,' said Dorothy, 'we seem to have got away without a hitch. Touch wood.' She tapped the dashboard.

'That's plastic,' observed her husband, Adrian, who was driving.

'Never mind,' said Dorothy, 'I'm not superstitious. By the way, what on earth were you doing half an hour ago? I looked out of the front bedroom window and saw you tearing off up the road in the car, and then about ten minutes later I looked out of the back bedroom window and you were in the garden, digging.'

'I'll tell you later,' said Adrian.

'That sounds suspicious,' said his eldest, Jonathan.

'What happened, Daddy?' asked Rosemary, the middle child.

'Try and guess,' said Adrian. 'It'll pass the time on the journey. Scene One: man dashes out of house, jumps into car loaded with holiday gear and drives off like a bat out of hell. Scene Two: ten minutes later, same man is observed digging in his back garden. Now what connection could there be between the two events?'

David Lodge

2 a Read the passage aloud by dividing the dialogue between the five characters and someone else reading the narrative in between. Observe the punctuation marks and read with appropriate intonation and pausing.

b This story opening is an example of a narrative which starts with a dialogue. What has the family been doing just before the story starts? Write a sentence to describe the actions of the family.

c Look at the seven underlined uses of *said* in Text 10A and with a partner try to think of other appropriate verbs which could be used instead.

3 a Working in pairs, find and list all the words in Text 10A which contain a short 'e' sound /e/, as in the word *set*. How many different letter combinations are there which produce this sound?

b With your partner, study the following words from Text 10A and say which are the two odd ones out, and why.

seat   gear   leaving   heavily   peace   inconvenience   between

c Still working with your partner, find words in Text 10A which contain a short 'u' sound /ʌ/, as in the word *cup*. Notice the different ways of spelling this sound. Can you think of some more?

4 a What do you think happened to Adrian? What are the clues to solving the mystery?

b Discuss the ways in which the story is ironic. How many examples of irony can you find?

c Can you infer what will happen to the family while they are on holiday? Why do you think so?

UNIT 10 Mysteries and puzzles

Key point

Inference

Good readers take in the explicit (explained and obvious) information given by a writer, and also notice the implicit (implied and not obvious) suggestions being made, so reading comprehension (understanding) has two levels. We can infer the solution to the mystery as long as we can pick up the clues in the text. The clues can take many forms, such as the choice of words, the way a character is described, the way they talk, the tone of the narrative voice. Sometimes one of the characters is naïve (unsuspecting) and we can guess things which they are not able to guess or have misunderstood. Even in a non-fiction text the attitude of the writer to the subject may be something which is implied, requiring reader inference.

Text 10B

This is the first part of a ballad, which tells of the search for three missing lighthouse keepers on a tiny remote island.

Flannan Isle

Though three men dwell on Flannan Isle
To keep the lamp alight,
As we steer'd **under the lee**, we caught
No **glimmer** through the night!

A passing ship at dawn had brought
The news; and quickly we set sail,
To find out what strange thing might ail
The keepers of the deep-sea light.

The winter day broke blue and bright,
With glancing sun and glancing spray,
While o'er the swell our boat made way,
As **gallant** as a gull in flight.

But, as we neared the lonely Isle;
And look'd up at the naked height;
And saw the lighthouse towering white,
With blinded lantern, that all night
Had never shot a spark
Of comfort through the dark,
So **ghostly** in the cold sunlight
It seem'd, that we were struck the while
With wonder all too **dread** for words.

And, as into the tiny creek
We stole beneath the hanging crag,
We saw three queer, black, ugly birds –
Too big, by far, in my belief,
For cormorant or shag –
Like seamen sitting bolt upright
Upon **a half-tide reef**:
But, as we neared, they plunged from sight,
Without a sound, or spurt of white.

And still too 'mazed to speak,
We landed; and **made fast** the boat;
And climbed the track in single file,
Each wishing he were safe afloat,
On any sea, however far,
So it be far from Flannan Isle:
And still we seemed to climb, and climb,
As though we'd lost all count of time,
And so must climb for evermore.
Yet, all too soon, we reached the door –
The black, sun-blister'd lighthouse door,
That gaped for us ajar.

As, on the **threshold**, for a spell,
We paused, we seemed to breathe the smell
Of limewash and of tar,
Familiar as our daily breath,
As though 'twere some strange scent of death:
And so, yet wondering, side by side,

UNIT 10 Mysteries and puzzles

We stood a moment, still tongue-tied:
And each with black foreboding eyed
The door, **ere** we should **fling** it wide,
To leave the sunlight for the gloom:
Till, plucking courage up, at last,
Hard on each other's heels we passed
Into the living-room.

Yet, as we crowded through the door,
We only saw a table, spread
For dinner, meat and cheese and bread;
But all untouch'd; and no one there:
As though, when they sat down to eat,
Ere they could even taste,
Alarm had come; and they in haste
Had risen and left the bread and meat:
For on the table-head a chair
Lay tumbled on the floor.

We listened; but we only heard
The **feeble** cheeping of a bird
That **starved** upon its perch:
And, listening still, without a word,
We set about our hopeless search.

Wilfrid Wilson Gibson

under the lee	out of the wind
a half-tide reef	a rock that is visible above the water only when the tide is halfway out
ere	before

5 a Which are the words which made the greatest impression on you when you read or heard Text 10B? Can you explain why?

b Find the words in Text 10B which have the following meanings.
  i   live (verb)
  ii trouble (verb)
  iii waves
  iv open (adjective)
  v   sense of misfortune

c Work with a partner. For each of the words in bold in Text 10B, choose the best synonym to fit the context. You may need to use a thesaurus.
  i   glimmer
  ii   gallant
  iii ghostly
  iv   dread
  v   made fast
  vi   threshold
  vii fling
  viii alarm
  ix   feeble
  x   starved

Cambridge Checkpoint English 7

Key point

Synonyms and vocabulary

The best synonym – which needs to be the same part of speech – may vary according to the exact context in which a word or phrase is being used. It is important to look at the surrounding words to be sure of choosing exactly the right meaning. A dictionary or thesaurus will offer several possibilities and you must take into account connotation (implied meaning) as well as denotation (literal meaning).

When considering words to use in your own writing, you should not simply accept the first word which comes to mind, as it is likely to be a cliché (overused expression, e.g. *it's high time, get a word in edgeways*) or an ordinary everyday word which only has a general meaning (e.g. *nice, bad*). Such vocabulary does not have much impact and will not be the most apt or subtle word. You also need to consider stylistic appropriateness, and even sound in some cases. The number of syllables in a word can be relevant to how formal or unusual it seems (e.g. *extraordinary* and *peculiar* are more interesting than *odd* and *strange*), and word length is especially relevant when writing poems, where it affects rhythm as well as voice.

6 a Text 10B is a ballad, which is a particular kind of poem. Look up the meaning of *ballad*, and then give examples of features of the poem which fit the definition.

b Discuss how the poem has built up suspense so far. Look at the description, and the order of the actions.

c Discuss how the reader has been made to feel sorry for the narrator of the poem. Pick out particular words which evoke the reader's sympathy.

7 a In small groups, pick out all the references to light in the poem, and discuss how the idea has been used and its effect.

b Still in your groups, look at the references to birds in the poem, and discuss what they imply.

c Discuss whether the searchers will find the three men. What do you think happened to them? What is the evidence from Text 10B which gives you this impression?

Text 10C

The listeners

'Is there anybody there?' said the Traveller,
  Knocking on the moonlit door;
And his horse in the silence champed the grasses
  Of the forest's ferny floor:
And a bird flew up out of the turret,
  Above the Traveller's head:
And he smote upon the door again a second time;
  'Is there anybody there?' he said.
But no one descended to the Traveller;
  No head from the leaf-fringed sill
Leaned over and looked into his grey eyes,
  Where he stood perplexed and still.
But only a host of phantom listeners
  That dwelt in the lone house then
Stood listening in the quiet of the moonlight
  To that voice from the world of men:
Stood thronging the faint moonbeams on the dark stair,
  That goes down to the empty hall,
Hearkening in an air stirred and shaken
  By the lonely Traveller's call.
And he felt in his heart their strangeness,
  Their stillness answering his cry,
While his horse moved, cropping the dark turf,
  'Neath the starred and leafy sky;
For he suddenly smote on the door, even
  Louder, and lifted his head:–
'Tell them I came, and no one answered,
  That I kept my word,' he said.
Never the least stir made the listeners,
  Though every word he spake
Fell echoing through the shadowiness of the still house
  From the one man left awake:
Ay, they heard his foot upon the stirrup,
  And the sound of iron on stone,
And how the silence surged softly backward,
  When the plunging hoofs were gone.

Walter De La Mare

8   a   Explain in one sentence of your own words what happens in the poem.
   b   How has the beginning of the poem been made intriguing, i.e. mysterious?

c Think of an explanation for what happens in the poem. You can turn this into a drama sketch to act out, once you have answered the following questions:
  i What is the house?
  ii Who is the Traveller?
  iii Who are the listeners?
  iv Why did the Traveller promise to go to the house?
  v Why don't the listeners answer his call?

Key point

Mysterious beginnings and endings

Texts 10A, 10B and 10C all begin in the middle of either a conversation or an action, but they are doing more than that; they are designed to intrigue (puzzle) or even shock readers as well as to engage them by jumping straight into the story. Readers are being presented with a mystery which they will want to solve. A powerful way to end a story is not to spell out what has happened or is going to happen, but to leave it to readers to draw their own conclusion. The story must provide the clues to make this withholding of explicit information possible.

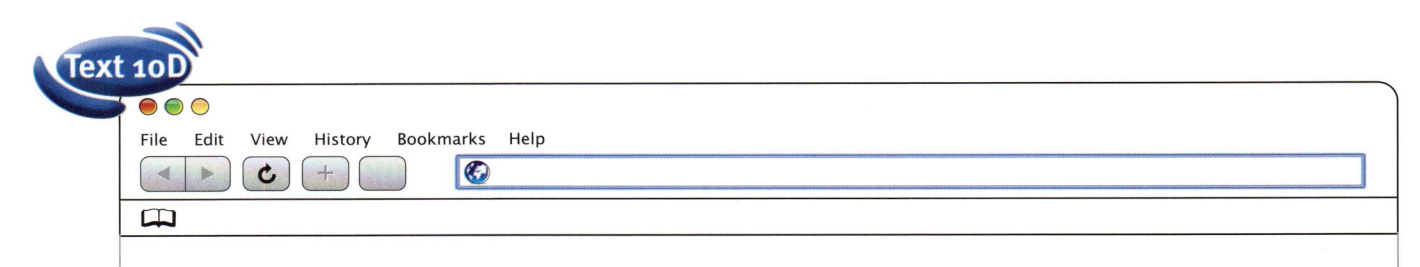

Text 10D

The *Mary Celeste*

On 5th December 1872 the captain of a ship called the *Dei Gratia*, on its way to Gibraltar from New York, saw a ship he recognised, called the *Mary Celeste*. The ship was moving strangely, although the sea was calm and her sails were up. Receiving no reply to his signal, Captain Morehouse drew his ship closer to the *Mary Celeste* and put men on board to investigate. There was nobody to be found. Although the ship was undamaged, and there were plenty of food supplies on board, the lifeboat was missing. The last log-book entry was dated ten days earlier, but gave no clue to the mysterious disappearance of the crew of the *Mary Celeste*.

UNIT 10 Mysteries and puzzles

9 Choose the correct answer for each of the multiple choice questions which follow.

  a Captain Morehouse
   i was not surprised to see the *Mary Celeste*.
   ii was surprised to see the *Mary Celeste*.
   iii was not surprised to see the *Mary Celeste* but was surprised by how it was moving.
   iv was surprised to see the *Mary Celeste*'s sails were up since the sea was calm.

  b The problem with the *Mary Celeste* was that
   i it had run out of food ten days earlier.
   ii something strange had happened ten days earlier.
   iii it had lost its lifeboat ten days earlier.
   iv it had suffered some damage ten days earlier.

  c The crew of the *Mary Celeste* did not reply to Captain Morehouse's signal because
   i they did not see it because they were not looking.
   ii they had been in a lifeboat for ten days.
   iii they did not recognise the *Dei Gratia*.
   iv they were not on board the ship.

10 **a** Working in small groups, discuss what you think might have happened to the crew of the *Mary Celeste*.

  b Look at the evidence in Text 10D and agree on a group view of what happened and why, and where they are now.

  c Nominate a member of your group to take on the role of Captain Morehouse and make a statement to the rest of the class of what your group think happened to the crew of the Mary Celeste, justifying your opinion.

  d In your groups, draft the script for a play to dramatise why the crew left their meal and abandoned the ship. Include stage directions to show the characters' movements.

  e Rehearse your play and perform it for the rest of the class.

11 Make up headlines for news reports based on the events in the three texts used in this unit.

  a Text 10A, Guess what happened

  b Text 10B, Flannan Isle

  c Text 10C, The *Mary Celeste*

Key point

Newspaper headlines

Headlines are a form of summary, and also a clue to the story which follows. Their aim is to arouse curiosity so you will pick up (and buy) the newspaper to read the full story. Headlines use as few words as possible – rarely more than five – to save space. They also use the shortest possible form of the word, which means active voice and present tense for past actions, and the infinitive for future actions (e.g. 'to go' not 'will go'). Old-fashioned and shorter words are also used, such as 'wed' and 'bid', and the shortest synonyms, so that catastrophes and disasters are called 'dramas', an increase is a 'rise' and a reduction is a 'fall'. If the story is shocking or dramatic, the headline may end in an exclamation mark or a question mark, e.g. 'Doomed!' or 'Whatever next?'.

12 During this unit you have looked at several stories which make use of puzzles, and one of them may have given you an idea for your own mystery story.

a List your possible ideas and, after considering them, highlight the one you think will make the most engaging story.

b Plan your story, paragraph by paragraph (you need about five) saying what will happen in each. It's very important to get the material in the right order so that clues are laid but not too much is given away, and suspense is built up.

c Write the first sentence to your story, using a shock or intrigue story opening, as in Text 10C. Write the last sentence to your story, leaving the final revelation or puzzle as late as possible by thinking about a delaying word order. For example, 'Amid the darkness and silence, watching from the bushes, was a gigantic and unrecognisable creature.'

d Draft your story, of about one and a half pages. If possible, type it on a computer, as this will allow you to improve the structure of your story by moving text around, as well as make corrections easily.

e When you are happy with your final version, read your story to the class or make an audio or video recording of it. First practise reading it at an appropriate pace (quite slowly, and using pauses in appropriate places for effect) and in a mysterious tone of voice.

UNIT 11 Looking back

In this unit you will reflect on people and events you remember, and see how memory and nostalgia can inspire personal reflective writing. You will learn how to use emotive language to get a response from readers, and how to write a character sketch. There will be practice in sentence structuring and drafting.

Activities

1
  a Make an 'I Remember . . .' list of ten things that you remember doing or owning in the past. For example, 'I remember when I went to the zoo and saw my first elephant' or 'I remember when I had a red baseball cap I wore everywhere'.

  b List ten things which don't exist any more but which were part of your childhood, such as television programmes, toys or sweets.

  c Look up the meaning of the word *nostalgia*. Discuss the idea in class, and give examples from your own life of times when you have felt this powerful emotion.

Text 11A is an extract from a blog called 'SayAfrica!' by the blogger Hunksam, who writes about rural life in his remote village over 20 years ago. It has American spelling.

Text 11A

Memories of an African childhood: school days

Waking up was not an easy task. My mom would drag me out of bed and toss me out of the house to a waiting basin of water to wash my face. Washing one's face before eating breakfast was such a cardinal rule in that household nobody ever skipped it. I have never known why. That done, we would herd around the hearth sipping tea.

My mom maintained such a serious countenance in the morning. You could easily earn a slap or a cooking stick on your tiny head at that particular time over a slight mistake. We took our breakfast with such quiet all you could hear was swigging and chewing sounds. Since school was near, the first bell would ring and the next would mean we were late.

When we woke early enough, we would wash our legs and arms (having washed our faces before breakfast), oil ourselves, sling our tiny bags on our backs and go running the short distance to school. My school bag was populated by only two exercise books: wide ruled for 'writing' and narrow ruled for 'math'. The other occupant of that school bag was a small piece of pencil. My pencils were made shorter by my gnawing habits when writing.

If you were late, you were stopped at the gate by the teacher on duty, made to kneel holding your ears and crawl the hundred meters to the assembly place thus. At the assembly, you were caned four strokes or five, or even ten, depending on the cruelty of that particular teacher.

At the assembly, we would sing the National Anthem and the Loyalty Pledge, pray, sing a hymn and be addressed by teachers. After that, they would check whether we had long nails. If you had long ones, you were given a good beating and sent home. Done with the assembly, we would run to class. There was an obsession with us kids to always run whenever we were going anywhere and be the first to get there and shout 'one', 'one'. The second one would shout 'two', 'two' and so forth. Whether going to the latrines, going out for breaks or coming back from lunch (we went home for lunch) we never walked. We always ran.

Another obsession of us kids was saying everything at the top of our voices. When asked your name, you would shout it out at the top of your voice. In my case then 'My name is Alfred Kiprotich Barusei Kenduiywo Kilachei . . .' Learning was by rote so we would shout everything after the teacher. 'Oneeee, twoooo, threeeee . . . Aaaa, Bbbb, Cccc, Dddd . . . aaaa, eee, iiii, ooo, uuu ad infinitum. The only pupil who was disadvantaged in this game was a friend of mine called Peter. He was such a stammerer that I never got to know his second name till he dropped out of school. He could faint trying to get a single syllable out.

The first lesson of the day was always Math which I loathed no end. We would go to the dusty road behind our school, clear a space each and write down our Math. 1, 2, 3, 4 . . . etc. Very big ones. The teacher would come and mark with his finger too. A long tick or a big cross. If not solving Math on the dirt road (there were no vehicles) we would count the sticks or bottle tops in class. We would also count our fingers and toes. That was Math.

I had a cousin, Stephen, who went by the nickname 'Tractor', maybe because he was huge. He was very good at Math but he hardly came to school. The reason why he stuck in my mind is because of his handwriting. When he was writing say a figure '1', he would draw such a big one that it would occupy the whole page. Ditto everything else. He finished his exercise

UNIT 11 Looking back

books in a day. He is now called '54', a very interesting fellow indeed.

The second lesson was English. We would sing A, B, C, D . . . the whole time. At times we would be given text books titled 'Tom and Mary'. This was my favorite subject. 'Tom and Mary' was an illustrated book about a family of Mr and Mrs Kamau. Mr Kamau was a school-bus driver. Mrs Kamau was a housewife. Tom and Mary were pupils. They had a little brother called Peter, a dog and a cat. I remember everything like yesterday because English was my favorite subject. We would sing about these stories after our teacher. We could not read so everything in our class was sung after the teacher:

'The man is Mr Kamau.'
'The woman is Mrs Kamau.'
'The boy is Tom.'
'The girl is Mary.'
'The baby is Peter.'
'The cat is drinking milk.'
And so on and so forth.

English tests involved 'filling in the missing words'. The 'a' in 'cat', the 'o' in 'boy' etc. It was very easy for me and I would score 100%. Did I tell you that we were categorized in rows according to cleverness? My row (I was brilliant except in Math) was called Lion, the next was Elephant and the dullest of us were called Giraffe. We sat on benches that were fixed to the ground.

The third lesson was Science. We just planted beans and maize in tins at the corner of our class. Our classes did not have doors or windows. Our plants would bend towards the light and that was Science for us! There was Home Science too. Other subjects were Mother-tongue, Swahili, Civics, History, Geography, Art and Craft, Music and Physical Education. They deserve a whole page each to describe.

2 a List the topics the writer refers to in Text 11A. These are all topics which you usually find in memoirs (writing about memories).

  b Can you say what the writer does to make the text more varied and interesting for the reader?

  c Which part of Text 11A did you find most appealing, and why?

3 a Find the ten words in Text 11A which have the following meanings. Write the words and their synonyms in your notebook.

| missed | collect | throw | expression | chewing |
| hated | gathering | endlessly | sorted | describe |

  b Text 11A is written mostly in simple sentences. Choose either the first or second paragraph and rewrite it in your notebook, joining the sentences with compound connectives (*and, but, so* and *or*) or relative connectives (*who* or *which*).

  c There are some groups of words between full stops in Text 11A which are not really sentences at all. Can you find them?

Cambridge Checkpoint English 7

Key point

Non-sentences

A sentence must contain a verb, and the verb must have a subject. Length is not important; 'Karim sang' is a sentence. You should write in sentences nearly all the time, but just occasionally, for dramatic effect, you may want to use only a single word, for example, 'Nothing.' This is most likely to happen at the end of a piece of writing. In dialogue you may also want to occasionally use a non-sentence to show something about the character speaking or the mood they are in. One of your characters could say, for example, 'Haven't a clue.' You are more likely to see examples of authors using non-sentences in informal and colloquial writing than in pieces in a formal style.

Text 11B

Learning with my grandfather

This is a boy's reflection on his relationship with his grandfather while growing up in Sudan.

I must have been very young at the time. While I don't remember exactly how old I was, I do remember that when people saw me with my grandfather they would pat me on the head and give my cheek a pinch – things they didn't do to my grandfather. The strange thing was that I never used to go out with my father, rather it was my grandfather who would take me with him wherever he went, except for the mornings when I would go to the mosque to learn the Koran. The mosque, the river and the fields – these were the landmarks in our life. While most of the children of my age grumbled at having to go to the mosque to learn the Koran, I used to love it. The reason was, no doubt, that I was quick at learning by heart and the Sheikh always asked me to stand up and recite the *Chapter of the Merciful* whenever we had visitors, who would pat me on my head and cheek just as people did when they saw me with my grandfather.

UNIT 11 Looking back

> Yes, I used to love the mosque, and I loved the river too. Directly we finished our Koran reading in the morning, I would throw down my wooden slate and dart off, quick as a genie, to my mother, hurriedly swallow down my breakfast, and run off for a plunge in the river. When tired of swimming about I would sit on the bank and gaze at the strip of water that wound away eastwards and hid behind a thick wood of acacia trees. I loved to give rein to my imagination and picture to myself a tribe of giants living behind that wood, a people tall and thin with white beards and sharp noses, like my grandfather. Before my grandfather ever replied to my many questions he would rub the tip of his nose with his forefinger; as for his beard, it was soft and luxuriant and as white as cotton-wool – never in my life have I seen anything of a purer whiteness or greater beauty.
>
> My grandfather must also have been extremely tall for I never saw anyone in the whole area address him without having to look up at him, nor did I see him enter a house without having to bend so low that I was put in mind of the way the river wound round behind the wood of acacia trees. I loved him and would imagine myself, when I grew to be a man, tall and slender like him, walking along with great strides.
>
> I believe I was his favourite grandchild: no wonder, for my cousins were a stupid bunch and I – so they say – was an intelligent child. I used to know when my grandfather wanted me to laugh, when to be silent; also I would remember the times for his prayers and would bring him his prayer-rug and fill the ewer for his ablutions without his having to ask me. When he had nothing else to do he enjoyed listening to me reciting to him from the Koran in a lilting voice, and I could tell from his face that he was moved.
>
> *From A Handful of Dates by Tayeb Salih*

4
a Why do you think adults patted the boy on the head and pinched his cheek?

b Find the following images in the passage and explain them in your own words.
  i quick as a genie
  ii give rein to my imagination
  iii tribe of giants

c Now write two short character descriptions, a paragraph for each one. In the first describe the character of the writer as a boy, in the second describe the character of the boy's grandfather. Use the tip on the next page to help you.

Tip

For Activity 4c
Writing a character sketch

When you are asked to write a character sketch, which is a task often required for the study of literary texts, you need to think of descriptive words which reveal the personality of the character (e.g. *wise, impatient, timid*). In order to make your interpretation of the character convincing, you should give evidence from the text to support it. This can be a quotation or a reference to something the character says or does. The sketch, which is a kind of picture in words, should be short and concise.

5 a On a copy of Text 11B, underline all the uses of *would* and *used to*. By using *would* or *used to* with a verb, the writer shows that the action took place regularly and uncountable times in the past. Write two sentences about your own past, one using *would* and the other using *used to*.

  b In pairs, look again at the following phrases from the passage.
  i <u>never in my life have I seen</u> anything of a purer whiteness or beauty
  ii <u>nor did I see</u> him enter a house without having to bend

  What do you notice about the word order in these two phrases? Agree with a partner what you think the rule is.

  c Find the four uses of a single dash in Text 11B. Can you remember how they are used? Look back at Activity 5 in Unit 9, page 115, which was about punctuation, if you need reminding.

6 Write an account, similar to Texts 11A and 11B, of a period of your life which was important in your growing up. Perhaps it was a time when someone came to live with you, you moved house, made a new friend, or took up a sport.

  a Collect your ideas as notes in a plan. Make sure to recall and include plenty of details, which is a way of making something ordinary seem special, and also making it engaging for the reader.

  b Draft a page of writing for your memoir. This means joining the notes together in full sentences and paragraphs, putting the ideas into a logical sequence. Use carefully chosen words, images and emotive language to suggest depth of feeling, which explains why it is still a strong memory for you. Read the key point about drafting to help you with this stage.

c Check and correct your draft, and then exchange with a partner for further improvement before writing (by hand or on a computer) the final version.

Key point

Drafting

There is a stage between making notes and producing a final version of a piece of writing, particularly one which is going to be assessed by a teacher or examiner. This stage is called drafting, and it is where you put your notes into full sentences, and link and sequence them in paragraphs. At this stage you also consider whether you have met the length requirement for the piece. If it is too long, you will have to remove repetitive or unnecessary material; if it is too short, you will have to add more ideas, information or detail. When you are reviewing and improving (editing) your draft, you should also consider whether you have used a wide enough range of vocabulary and sentence types, and whether your style of writing is suitable for the task. This is also an opportunity to correct any errors of spelling, punctuation and grammar which you notice. The final version will then be better than the draft version in several ways.

The next part of the unit looks at two nostalgia poems.

7 a Read the poem 'Piano' in Text 11C on the next page. In one sentence, say where the persona is and what is happening.

b What is the poem saying about music?

c Look at the following aspects of the poem, and then say in one sentence each what effect they have on the feeling of the poem and on how you respond to it.
    i the length of the lines
    ii the rhyme scheme
    iii the run-on lines
    iv the repeated words
    v the last line

Text 11C

Piano

Softly, in the dusk, a woman is singing to me;
Taking me back down the vista of years, till I see
A child sitting under the piano, in the boom of the tingling strings
And pressing the small, poised feet of a mother who smiles as she sings.

In spite of myself, the insidious mastery of song
Betrays me back, till the heart of me weeps to belong
To the old Sunday evenings at home, with winter outside
And hymns in the cosy parlour, the tinkling piano our guide.

So now it is vain for the singer to burst into clamour
With the great black piano appassionato. The glamour
Of childish days is upon me, my manhood is cast
Down in the flood of remembrance, I weep like a child for the past.

D.H. Lawrence

Key point

Poem endings

Poems nearly always have a very important last line or pair of lines, which contain the moral or message of the whole poem. The reader has been prepared for it, and yet there can also be a feeling of surprise at the power of the emotion suddenly released. This is often emphasised by the final lines being a couplet (rhyming pair), or by introducing a gap before the last line or lines. The next poem makes use of this form to emphasise the sense of nostalgia and loss.

Text 11D

The tarantella is a whirling southern Italian dance once thought to be a remedy for the bite of a tarantula spider.

Tarantella

Do you remember an Inn,
Miranda?
Do you remember an Inn?
And the **tedding** and the spreading
Of the straw for a bedding,
And the fleas that tease in the High Pyrenees,
And the wine that tasted of tar?
And the cheers and the jeers of the young **muleteers**
(Under the vine of the dark veranda)?
Do you remember an Inn, Miranda,
Do you remember an Inn?
And the cheers and the jeers of the young muleteers
Who hadn't got a penny,
And who weren't paying any,
And the hammer at the doors and the din?
And the hip! hop! hap!
Of the clap
Of the hands to the swirl and the twirl
Of the girl gone chancing,
Glancing,
Dancing,
Backing and advancing,
Snapping of the clapper to the spin
Out and in –
And the ting, tong, tang of the guitar!
Do you remember an Inn,
Miranda?
Do you remember an Inn?

Never more;
Miranda,
Never more.
Only the high peaks **hoar**;
And Aragon a torrent at the door.
No sound
In the walls of the halls where falls
The tread

Of the feet of the dead to the ground,
No sound:

But the boom
Of the far waterfall like doom.

Hilaire Belloc

tedding	turning over the straw to make a sort of mattress
muleteer	someone who looks after mules; a mule is an animal that is half-donkey, half-horse
hoar	frosty

8 On a copy of Text 11D, and working with a partner, underline and comment on how the following aspects of the poem affect its rhythm.

  a the variation of line lengths

  b the internal rhyme within lines

  c the use of questions

9 In this activity you are going to write your own rhythm poem. First think of what your poem will be about. It must be something that has a strong and distinctive sound or movement – a train, a galloping horse, a fairground ride or a kind of music, for example.

  a Now make decisions and notes about the following three ways to represent sound and movement.
   i line length
   ii metre
   iii rhyme

  b Draft your poem, and give it a suitable title.

  c Read your poem aloud, clearly conveying its rhythm.

In the next part of the unit, you are going to read two letters of confession. There is a radio show in the UK called *Confessions*, hosted by Simon Mayo, to which people write letters admitting to things they did when they were much younger which they feel guilty about and want to be forgiven for.

Text 11E

Dear Simon

I'm so glad you have started a confessional service, because it allows me to admit something I did which I've never had the courage to confess before. Some twelve years ago, I did an awful thing. You see, being the grand old age of ten, I felt that my bicycle was too small and babyish for me. To give you some idea what this bike was like, it was called a 'Zippy'. Well, I nagged and nagged my parents for a new bike, but to no avail. Their argument was that there was nothing wrong with the one I had, and I could wait a few years before I got a new one. All I could think about was getting a new bike, so I decided to take things into my own hands. I had noticed that behind the local shops it was very overgrown with weeds and nettles about knee high. Every time I was sent to the shops to fetch something for my mother, I would remove something from my bike. I began to dismantle it bit by bit. Each week a nut or bolt or screw would mysteriously disappear, until finally, one day, I arrived home pushing what was left of my bike. I pretended to be most distraught and told my parents that somehow my bike had just simply fallen apart. I must have been convincing because they believed me. Sure enough, my wicked plan worked and a week later I was presented with a brand new grown-up bike. I am feeling really awful about this now and I've never admitted what terrible lengths I went to so I would get a new bike. We have since moved, but if anyone ever develops the piece of land behind the shops, they will come across enough bike parts to build a new one! I'm sorry, Mum and Dad. I hope I can be forgiven.

Karen

10 You will need a copy of Text 11E for this activity.

  a First read the letter in Text 11E and put paragraph breaks in suitable places on your copy of it.

  b All the punctuation has been removed from the following extract from Text 11E. Without looking back at the text, put full stops, commas and capital letters in a copy of the extract below. Then check your version with the original.

  > All I could think about was getting a new bike so I decided to take things into my own hands I had noticed that behind the local shops it was very overgrown with weeds and nettles about knee high every time I was sent to the shops to fetch something for my mother I would remove something from my bike I began to dismantle it bit by bit each week a nut or bolt or screw would mysteriously disappear until finally one day I arrived home pushing what was left of my bike

  c Highlight the verbs which can be contracted in a copy of the extract below, and put apostrophes for omission in the correct places. For example, *I am* can become *I'm*.

  > I am feeling really awful about this now and I have never admitted what terrible lengths I went to so I would get a new bike. We have since moved, but if anyone ever develops the piece of land behind the shops, they will come across enough bike parts to build a new one!

Text 11F

Dear Simon

I have a dreadful confession to make. Seven years ago, aged thirteen, I used to live in a <u>cul-de-sac</u>. My friends who lived in the street used to get up to various <u>pranks</u>, but nothing compared to what happened one hot summer's day. It hadn't rained for weeks and we were sitting on a grass bank, wondering what mischief we could get up to.
Finally, one of the gang suggested that we light a fire. This was agreed, so we each went home to collect items to burn. I went to call on James, a friend of mine, but he wasn't allowed out by his mother because of an incident he had just caused at the supermarket.

We piled the old newspapers and litter together, poured on some oil, and lit the fire. Before long, we had a nice <u>blaze</u> going. However, when we added more oil to it, it got out of control. We tried to put the fire out, but only succeeded in setting a nearby tree alight. As it <u>erupted</u>, we realised that we were going to be in trouble and ran off. I found my mother and told her that there was a fire across the road. While she rang the emergency number, I looked out of the window and watched the flames <u>envelop</u> the end of a neighbour's garden.

At this point, James, having been sent to his room in disgrace, looked out of his window and saw the fire. He shinned down the drainpipe outside his bedroom window and rushed towards the fire with the blanket from his bed. He threw it over the blaze and jumped back as it too went up in flames. As he tried desperately to put out the fire, it reached the caravan parked in the neighbour's garden, and it was soon burning furiously too. At this point, a fire engine and a police car arrived. The police officer grabbed James and pulled him towards the car, since he thought that James had started it. Unfortunately for James, a number of witnesses stated that they had seen him burning a blanket, which confirmed the police officer's suspicions.

The fire brigade finally managed to put out the fire just before the neighbour's house caught fire, but his caravan was completely destroyed. Since James

> was only ten at the time, he got away with a severe warning from the police and another punishment from his parents.
> To this day, James does not know how the fire started, but I now feel the time has come to confess.
> Yours sincerely
>
> Dave

11 a Use the following underlined words from Text 11F in a sentence each to show you understand their meaning.

cul-de-sac   prank   blaze   erupted   envelop

b In pairs, discuss and write a one-sentence explanation for why the word *mischief* is spelt with *ie* but *neighbour* is spelt with *ei*.

c There are ten irregular past tense verbs in the text. Find them all and give the present tense form of each one. Read the key point about irregular verbs to help you.

Key point

Irregular past simple verbs

- Most of the verbs in English, and in Text 11F, are regular, which means they form their past tense using *ed* (e.g. *allowed*). The preceding consonant will be double if the vowel is short (e.g. *grabbed*). If the verb ends in a *y* which is pronounced as a syllable (e.g. *try* or *carry*, but not *obey*), then the *y* changes to an *i* before the *ed* is added (e.g. *tried*, *carried*).
- There is a group of verbs which have optional past tense forms, because there exist older and newer versions. They can take either *ed* or *t* in the past tense. Examples of this kind are *leap*, *spell* and *burn*, which have the past tense forms *leaped/leapt*, *spelled/spelt* and *burned/burnt*. The *t* (i.e. the irregular) version is the more modern spelling/pronunciation.
- The most commonly used verbs in English are irregular (e.g. *have*, *come* and *do*). Some form their past simple tense by changing the vowel (e.g. *sing* → *sang*, *keep* → *kept*). Others undergo even more of a change to form the past tense (e.g. *buy* → *bought*, *go* → *went*).

UNIT 11 Looking back

> - Another category of commonly used verbs do not change their form, regardless of the tense (e.g. *read, put*).
>
> Irregular verbs have to be learnt so that you can recognise them in your reading and use them in your writing, correctly spelt, without having to think about them.

12 You are going to write your own confession to be broadcast on a radio programme.

  a Write a draft of your letter, starting 'Dear Simon . . .' Use the tip below to help you.

  b Use emotive language to make the reader/listener feel sympathy for you and inclined to forgive you.

  c Check the paragraphing, use of full stops, commas and apostrophes in your letter.

Tip

For Activity 12a
Confessing

Think of something you did and got away with in the past which you now wish to own up for. If you can't think of a real thing, borrow an idea from a film or something which you know has happened to someone else. For instance, you broke a vase and blamed the cat, or you made up a false excuse for the teacher about why you hadn't revised for the exam. It is better if there is some drama and/or irony involved. In Text 11F, the irony is that the person who tried to put out the fire was the one who got the blame for starting it! Because it is an informal letter, representing a spoken confession, it can use contractions of verb forms (e.g. *I'm, shouldn't*).

To finish this unit, you will look at one more poem on the theme of remembering and then write your own.

It was long ago

I'll tell you, shall I, something I remember?
Something that still means a great deal to me.
It was long ago.

A dusty road in summer I remember,
A mountain, and an old house, and a tree
That stood, you know,

Behind the house. An old woman I remember
In a red shawl with a grey cat on her knee
Humming under a tree.

She seemed the oldest thing I can remember,
But then perhaps I was not more than three.
It was long ago.

I dragged on the dusty road, and I remember
How the old woman looked over the fence at me
And seemed to know

How it felt to be three, and called out, I remember
'Do you like bilberries and cream for tea?'
I went under the tree

UNIT 11 Looking back

And while she hummed, and the cat purred, I remember
How she filled a saucer with berries and cream for me
So long ago,

Such berries and such cream as I remember
I never had seen before and never see
Today, you know.

And that is almost all I can remember,
The house, the mountain, the grey cat on her knee,
Her red shawl, and the tree,

And the taste of the berries, the feel of the sun I remember,
And the smell of everything that used to be
So long ago,

Till the heat on the road outside again I remember,
And how the long dusty road seemed to have for me
No end, you know.

That is the farthest thing I can remember.
It won't mean much to you. It does to me.
Then I grew up, you see.

Eleanor Farjeon

13 Discuss the poem in Text 11G with a partner and say why you think the poem:

   a uses very simple words, many of them of only one syllable

   b uses repetition of words and whole phrases

   c addresses the reader directly as 'you'.

14 Write your own poem called 'It was long ago', which describes an early memory very simply, using the same format and devices as in Text 11G. Use the tip on the next page to help you.

For Activity 14
Composing your poem

Study the 'It was long ago' poem in Text 11G again, and notice that:
- the first line of each three-line verse ends in 'remember'
- the second line ends with either 'me' or a word that rhymes with 'me'
- the third line ends with 'ago' or another reference to time
- there are run-on verses in the middle of the poem
- the poem begins and ends with quiet reflection, in contrast to the emotion in the middle section as the speaker's memory carries her away.

Although it is generally not a good idea to begin sentences and poetry lines with 'And', it can be effective in reflective writing to show how the persona is returning to a childish way of expressing themselves, and how the memory is flooding back and has to be listed in order to be captured. You can address the reader as 'you' if you wish, in order to involve them and make it sound as though you are confiding in them, as well as warning them that it will happen to them too, when they grow up.

UNIT 12 Secret lives

In this unit you will look at examples of how dreams and daydream fantasies have been used in stories and poems. You will practise supporting your views, the formation of comparative and superlative adjectives, and more punctuation of dialogue. You will also write a reflective poem.

Activities

1
  a Why do we have daydreams? What do you daydream about? Tell your partner.

  b Write three wishes on a piece of paper and swap it with a partner. Are they the same or different? Discuss why.

  c If you could travel anywhere in the world, where would you want to go, and why? Tell the class.

Text 12A

Pool of tears

This is an extract from *Alice's Adventures in Wonderland* by Lewis Carroll. In Alice's dream she has fallen down a rabbit hole and eaten a cake which has made her grow so tall that she cannot get through a small gate into a garden.

'Curiouser and curiouser!' cried Alice (she was so much surprised, that for the moment she quite forgot how to speak good English); 'now I'm opening out like the largest telescope that ever was! Good-bye, feet!' (for when she looked down at her feet, they seemed to be almost out of sight, they were getting so far off). 'Oh, my poor little feet, I wonder who will put on your shoes and stockings for you now, dears? I'm sure *I* shan't be able! I shall be a great deal too far off to trouble myself about you: you must manage the best way you can; but I must be kind to them,' thought Alice, 'or perhaps they won't walk the way I want to go! Let me see: I'll give them a new pair of boots every Christmas.'

And she went on planning to herself how she would manage it. 'They must go by the carrier,' she thought; 'and how funny it'll seem, sending presents to one's own feet! And how odd the directions will look!

Alice's Right Foot, Esq.
Hearthrug,
near the Fender,
(with Alice's love).

Oh dear, what nonsense I'm talking!'

Just then her head struck against the roof of the hall: in fact she was now more than nine feet high, and she at once took up the little golden key and hurried off to the garden door. Poor Alice! It was as much as she could do, lying down on one side, to look through into the garden with one eye; but to get through was more hopeless than ever: she sat down and began to cry again.

'You ought to be ashamed of yourself,' said Alice, 'a great girl like you,' (she might well say this), 'to go on crying in this way! Stop this moment, I tell you!' But she went on all the same, shedding gallons of tears, until there was a large pool all round her, about four inches deep and reaching half down the hall.

After a time she heard a little pattering of feet in the distance, and she hastily dried her eyes to see what was coming. It was the White Rabbit returning, splendidly dressed, with a pair of white kid gloves in one hand and a large fan in the other: he came trotting along in a great hurry, muttering to himself as he came, 'Oh! the Duchess, the Duchess! Oh! won't she be savage if I've kept her waiting!'

Alice felt so desperate that she was ready to ask help of any one; so, when the Rabbit came near her, she began, in a low, timid voice, 'If you please, sir –' The Rabbit started violently, dropped the white kid gloves and the fan, and scurried away into the darkness as hard as he could go. Alice took up the fan and gloves, and, as the hall was very hot, she kept fanning herself all the time she went on talking: 'Dear, dear! How queer everything is today! And yesterday things went on just as usual. I wonder if I've been changed in the night? Let me think: was I the same when I got up this morning? I almost think I can remember feeling a little different. But if I'm not the same, the next question is, Who in the world am I? Ah, *that's* the great puzzle!'

UNIT 12 Secret lives

2 **a** Dreams have characteristics which make them different from reality. In pairs, list all the ways you can tell that Text 12A is a dream story.

b In Text 12A Alice talks to herself. Why do you think the writer made her do this? Discuss the possible reasons with your partner.

c If this were your story, what would you make happen next to Alice? Share your idea with your partner and decide which is the best.

3 **a** Alice 'quite forgot how to speak good English' when she said 'Curiouser and curiouser'. What is wrong with this phrase? Write what Alice should have said.

b Discuss the formation of comparative adjectives with a partner. For example, why is *happier* the comparative form of *happy*, but *more hopeless* the comparative form of *hopeless*? Copy the table below into your notebook and list five more examples of adjectives which don't use *more*, and five more examples of those which do, in the comparative form. Read the key point below about the comparative and superlative forms of adjectives to help you.

One-word comparative adjectives	Comparative adjectives with *more*
happy – *happier*	hopeless – *more hopeless*

c Adjectives also have a superlative form, to describe the most … of many, as in 'the largest telescope that ever was', 'the most frightening sight she had ever seen'. Give the superlative of the following adjectives, taking care with spelling:

| beautiful | kind | timid | good | hot |
| splendid | savage | desperate | hard | bad |

Key point

Comparative and superlative adjectival forms

The adjective usually takes the suffix *er* for the comparative form (e.g. *this is grander than that*) and *est* for the superlative form (e.g. *this is the grandest of all*). However, if the adjective already has more than two syllables, like *curious*, then the comparative is formed with *more* plus the adjective (*more curious*), and the superlative with *most* plus the adjective (*most curious*). Remember if the adjective ends in a stressed *y*, this will change to an *i* (e.g. *prettier, windiest*), and if the vowel is short, the consonant will double (e.g. *bigger, hottest*). Note that for adjectives ending in *ed, ing, ful* or *less*, we always use *more* and *most* rather than add another suffix to the word (e.g. *more boring, most worried*).

Text 12B

Like Text 12A, this extract comes from *Alice's Adventures in Wonderland*, a few pages further on when Alice converses with a mouse which has fallen into the pool of her tears.

The Mouse gave a sudden leap out of the water, and seemed to quiver all over with fright. Oh, I beg your pardon! cried Alice hastily, afraid that she had hurt the poor animal's feelings. I quite forgot you didnt like cats. Not like cats! cried the Mouse, in a shrill, passionate voice. Would *you* like cats if you were me? Well, perhaps not, said Alice in a soothing tone: dont be angry about it. And yet I wish I could show you our cat Dinah: I think youd take a fancy to cats if you could only see her. She is such a dear quiet thing, Alice went on, half to herself, as she swam lazily about in the pool, and she sits purring so nicely by the fire, licking her paws and washing her face – and shes such a nice soft thing to nurse – and shes such a capital one for catching mice – oh, I beg your pardon! cried Alice again, for this time the Mouse was bristling all over, and she felt certain it must be really offended. We wont talk about her any more if youd rather not. We indeed! cried the Mouse, who was trembling down to the end of his tail. As if *I* would talk on such a subject! Our family always *hated* cats: nasty, low, vulgar things! Dont let me hear the name again! I wont indeed! said Alice, in a great hurry to change the subject of conversation.

4 You will need a copy of Text 12B for this activity. Did you have any difficulty reading the passage? Was it because some of the punctuation is missing?

  a You will have noticed that the speech marks have been removed from Text 12B. On your copy of the text, put them in to show the beginnings and ends of all the speeches.

  b When the speaker changes, the paragraph must also change. Show the beginnings of new lines (use //).

  c The apostrophes have also been removed from the passage. Replace the ten which are missing.

Text 12C

This poem is about being transported to a magical dream world which becomes more real than reality.

Romance

When I was but thirteen or so
I went into a golden land,
Chimborazo, Cotopaxi,
Took me by the hand.

My father died, my brother too,
They passed like fleeting dreams,
I stood where Popocatapetl
In the sunlight gleams.

I dimly heard the master's voice
And boys far-off at play,
Chimborazo, Cotopaxi
Had stolen me away.

I walked in a great golden dream
To and fro from school –
Shining Popocatapetl
The dusty streets did rule.

I walked home with a gold dark boy
And never a word I'd say,
Chimborazo, Cotopaxi
Had taken my speech away.

I gazed entranced upon his face
Fairer than any flower –
O shining Popocatepetl
It was thy magic hour:

The houses, people, traffic seemed
Thin, fading dreams by day,
Chimborazo, Cotopaxi
They had stolen my soul away.

W.J. Turner

5 **a** Write and then say out loud the names of the Mexican volcanoes in the poem. What are the unusual letters and sounds which make the words sound so magical? Can you think of similar place names which have the same effect?

b In another famous poem, the place names used are Xanadu, Alph, Abyssinian. Which vowel sound, also used in Text 12C, seems to be the one which is considered to be the most exotic? Think of the place name Samarkand and the magic word Abracadabra!

c Make up three words which could be the names of exotic countries, mountains or rivers, using the consonants and vowel referred to in 5a and 5b above.

Text 12D

The strange host

Text 12D comes from *Dracula* by Bram Stoker, in which the visitor to Count Dracula's castle in Romania comes to believe that his host is living a secret life.

8 May
I only slept a few hours when I went to bed, and feeling that I could not sleep any more, got up. I had hung my shaving glass by the window, and was just beginning to shave. Suddenly I felt a hand on my shoulder, and heard the Count's voice saying to me, 'Good morning.' I **started**, for it amazed me that I had not seen him, since the reflection of the glass covered the whole room behind me. In starting I had cut myself slightly, but did not notice it at the moment. Having answered the Count's **salutation**, I turned to the glass again to see how I had been mistaken. This time there could be no error, for the man was close to me, and I could see him over my shoulder. But there was no reflection of him in the mirror! The whole room behind me was displayed, but there was no sign of a man in it, except myself.

This was startling, and coming on the top of so many strange things, was beginning to increase that vague feeling of uneasiness which I always have when the Count is near. But at the instant I saw that the cut had bled a little, and the blood was trickling over my chin. I laid down the razor, turning as I did so half round to look for some sticking plaster. When the Count saw my face, his eyes blazed with a sort of demoniac fury, and he suddenly made a grab at my throat.

UNIT 12 Secret lives

'Take care,' he said, 'take care how you cut yourself. It is more dangerous than you think in this country.' Then seizing the shaving glass, he went on, 'And this is the **wretched** thing that has done the mischief. It is a foul **bauble** of man's vanity. Away with it!' And opening the window with one wrench of his terrible hand, he flung out the glass, which was shattered into a thousand pieces on the stones of the courtyard far below. Then he withdrew without a word. It is very annoying, for I do not see how I am to shave, unless in my watch-case or the bottom of the shaving pot, which is fortunately of metal.

When I went into the dining room, breakfast was prepared, but I could not find the Count anywhere. So I breakfasted alone. It is strange that as yet I have not seen the Count eat or drink. He must be a very peculiar man! After breakfast I did a little exploring in the castle. I went out on the stairs, and found a room looking towards the South.

The view was magnificent, and from where I stood there was every opportunity of seeing it. The castle is on the very edge of a terrible precipice. A stone falling from the window would fall a thousand feet without touching anything! As far as the eye can reach is a sea of green tree tops, with occasionally a deep rift where there is a chasm. Here and there are silver threads where the rivers wind in deep gorges through the forests.

But I am not in heart to describe beauty, for when I had seen the view I explored further. Doors, doors, doors everywhere, and all locked and bolted. In no place save from the windows in the castle walls is there an available exit. The castle is a **veritable** prison, and I am a prisoner!

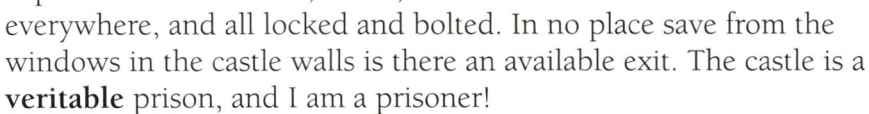

6 As you read Text 12D, you will probably notice that the language is old-fashioned. This activity focuses on the vocabulary used in the piece.

   a Replace the five slightly archaic words in bold in the text with a synonym for each. If you don't know their meaning, guess first before using a dictionary.

b Now change the three phrases below into your own words.
- he withdrew without a word
- on the very edge of a terrible precipice
- I am not in heart

c Replace this direct speech by the Count with reported speech:

'Take care,' he said, 'take care how you cut yourself. It is more dangerous than you think in this country.'

7 Write three paragraphs which answer the following three questions, giving three pieces of evidence for each.

What are the clues in Text 12D that:

a there is something odd and inhuman about the Count?

b there is something scary about the castle and its setting?

c something horrific will happen in the story?

8 a List some adjectives or nouns of your own which describe the character of the Count.

b Write a sentence to summarise how you think the story will develop.

Text 12E

I'd rather be …

I'd rather be a sparrow than a snail.
Yes I would.
If I only could,
I surely would.

I'd rather be a hammer than a nail.
Yes I would.
If I only could,
I surely would.

Chorus
Away, I'd rather sail away,
Like a swan that's here and gone.
A man gets tied up to the ground,
He gives the world

UNIT 12 Secret lives

> Its saddest sound,
> Its saddest sound.
>
> I'd rather be a forest than a street.
> Yes I would.
> If I only could,
> I surely would.
>
> I'd rather feel the earth beneath my feet,
> Yes I would.
> If I only could,
> I surely would.
>
> *Paul Simon and Jorge Milchberg*

9 You might have guessed that Text 12D contains the words of a song, which are called lyrics because most songs express personal feelings.

   a Discuss in class why someone would rather be:
   - a sparrow than a snail
   - a hammer than a nail
   - a forest than a street.

   b Write in your own words what you think 'A man gets tied up to the ground' means.

   c Write a new first verse for the song, using the same format and metre. Read or sing it to the class.

Text 12F

Vocation

When the gong sounds at ten in the morning and I walk to school by our lane,
Every day I meet the hawker crying, 'Bangles, crystal bangles!'
There is nothing to hurry him on, there is no road he must take, no place he must go to, no time when he must come home.
I wish I were a hawker, spending my day in the road, crying, 'Bangles, crystal bangles!'

When at four in the afternoon I come back from the school,
I can see through the gate of that house the gardener digging the ground.

He does what he likes with his spade, he soils his clothes
    with the dust,
Nobody takes him to task if he gets baked in the sun or
    gets wet.
I wish I were a gardener digging away at the garden with
    nobody to stop me from digging.

Just as it gets dark in the evening and my mother sends me
    to bed,
I can see through my open window the watchman walking
    up and down.
The lane is dark and lonely, and the street-lamp stands
Like a giant with one red eye in its head.

The watchman swings his lantern and walks with his
    shadow at his side, and never once goes to bed in his life.
I wish I were a watchman walking the streets all night,
    chasing the shadows with my lantern.

Rabindranath Tagore

10 In small groups, study the poem in Text 12F and answer the following questions to feedback to the rest of the class.

 a How would you describe the kind of people that the writer envies?

 b Why do you think the lines are so long (some do not fit onto the width of a page).

 c What can you say about the form of the poem? Is there anything regular about it? In what senses would you call it a poem?

Key point

'I were'

The usage 'I were' is an example of a verb in the subjunctive form, which is rarely used in English. It shows that what is being said is not true and is just the expression of a wish or speculation. We also say, 'If I were you …' rather than 'If I was you …', so do not be surprised to come across this usage, which exists in many other languages.

UNIT 12 Secret lives

11
a Write three sentences beginning 'I wish I were …', choosing jobs you are fascinated by and think you would like to do. Look at the key point about 'I were' to help you.

b Now turn your three sentences into three verses using Text 12F as a model, with each final line beginning 'I wish I were …' Use the tip below to help you write your verses.

c Put the verses into the best order. Check and improve the content, style and accuracy of your poem. Write it out neatly and illustrate it for display in the classroom.

Tip

For Activity 11b
Writing a 'I wish I were …' poem

The poem you are writing is in free verse. Although it is loosely divided into verses, they do not have a fixed form; there is no rhyme scheme, no metre, no regular number of lines. The poem in Text 12F does have imagery, and you should use some in your poem. In Rabindranath Tagore's poem, the repetitions and simple vocabulary convey the idea that it is a child speaking. The present tense makes the poem seem to be a spontaneous series of reflections of something being witnessed and recorded. Notice how the poem is given a structure by the use of the changing time of day, from ten in the morning to bedtime. You can adopt this structure for your own poem if you like.

Acknowledgements

Marian Cox and Cambridge University Press would like to express their gratitude to Chrissie Sims for her good work on the interactive questions on the Cambridge Elevate enhanced edition of the Coursebook.

The authors and publishers acknowledge the following sources of copyright material and are grateful for the permissions granted. While every effort has been made, it has not always been possible to identify the sources of all the material used, or to trace all copyright holders. If any omissions are brought to our notice, we will be happy to include the appropriate acknowledgements on reprinting.

p. 6 from *The Story of My Life* by Helen Keller, copyright © 2012 by Helen Keller, used by permission of the American Foundation for the Blind Helen Keller Archives, all rights reserved; pp. 8, 10, 44 from *Cider with Rosie* by Laurie Lee, published by Vintage Books, reprinted by permission of The Random House Group Ltd and United agents on behalf of the Estate of Laurie Lee; p. 13 'Jim' from *Cautionary Verses* by Hilaire Belloc © Hilaire Belloc reprinted by permission of Peters Fraser & Dunlop (www.petersfraserdunlop.com) on behalf of the estate of Hilaire Belloc; p. 19 from *The Book of Mini-sagas Vol. III*, © Telegraph Media Group Limited, 1988; p. 26 'My Favourite Things' by Richard Rodgers & Oscar Hammerstein II, copyright © 1959 by Richard Rodgers & Oscar Hammerstein II, copyright renewed, International copyright secured, all rights reserved, used by permission of Williamson Music, a division of Rodgers & Hammerstein: an Imagem Company; p. 35 'Autumn for me is' by Helen Mackay, from *Weathers and Seasons*, Evans Brothers Ltd, 1974; p. 41 from *The Endless Steppe* by Esther Hautzig, copyright © Esther Hautzig, reprinted by permission of A.M. Heath & Co. Ltd; p. 46 'What is a teacher?' by Gerald Grow, www.longleaf.net; p. 47 'First Day at School' by Roger McGough from *In the Glassroom* (© Roger McGough 1976) is reprinted by permission of United Agents (www.unitedagents.co.uk) on behalf of Roger McGough; p. 48 from *Boy, Tales of Childhood* by Roald Dahl; p. 60 from *Jonathan Livingston Seagull* by Richard Bach, used with kind permission of the author; p. 61 from 'His First Flight' from *Liam O'Flaherty: The Collected Stories Volume 1* by Liam O'Flaherty reprinted by permission of Peters Fraser & Dunlop (www.petersfraserdunlop.com) on behalf of the Estate of Liam O'Flaherty; p. 63 'On Eagle's Wings' by Mark S. Bubien, used with permission; p. 70 adapted from 'Telani Rama the Messenger' by Brishti Bandyopadhyay © Pitara.com; p. 83 'A Rattling Experience' by Richard Grant reproduced with permission of Curtis Brown Group Ltd, London on behalf of Richard Grant, copyright © Richard Grant 1995; p. 88 from *My Family and Other Animals* by Gerald Durrell reproduced with permission of Curtis Brown Group Ltd, London on behalf of the Estate of Gerald Durrell, copyright © The Estate of Gerald Durrell, 1956; p. 93 from *Walkabout* by James Vance Marshall, retold by Gillian Porter Ladousse (first published as *The Children* by Michael Joseph 1959, Penguin Readers version Pearson Education 2000), copyright © James Vance Marshall, 1969, reproduced by permission of Penguin Books Ltd, Sundance/Newbridge Publishing, and Johnson & Alcock; p. 110 'A goddess can't call her life her own' by Clare Harvey from The Sunday Times Magazine, November 2011 © NI Syndication; p. 114 from *Family Talk* by Rex Harley, used with kind permission of the author; p. 119 'Presents from My Aunts in Pakistan' by Moniza Alvi from *Split World: Poems 1990-2005* (Bloodaxe Books, 2008); p. 122 'My Grandmother' by Elizabeth Jennings from *New Collected Poems*, Carcanet, with permission from David Higham Associates; p. 125 'Guess what happened' from *Working with Structuralism* by David Lodge, reproduced with permission of Curtis Brown Group Ltd, London on behalf of David Lodge, copyright © David Lodge 1981; p. 127 'Flannan Isle' from *Collected Poems* by Wilfred Gibson, Pan Macmillan, London, copyright © Wilfred Gibson, 1926; p. 131 'The Listeners' by Walter de la Mare, used with permission of The Literary Trustees of Walter de la Mare and The Society of Authors as their representative; p. 135 'Memories of an African Childhood' from SayAfrica.blogspot.com, by K.B. Samoei, used with kind permission of the author; p. 138 from 'A Handful of Dates' from *The Wedding of Zein* by Tayeb Salih, © Tayeb Salih used by permission of United Agents Ltd (www.unitedagents.co.uk) on behalf of the author; p. 143 'Tarantella' from *Sonnets and Verse* by Hilaire Belloc © Hilaire Belloc reprinted by permission of Peters Fraser & Dunlop (www.petersfraserdunlop.com) on behalf of the Estate of Hilaire Belloc; pp. 145, 146 from *Confessions* by Simon Mayo, Marshall Pickering, 1991; p. 150 'It was Long Ago' by Eleanor Farjeon from *Morning Has Broken*, Macmillan, with permission from David Higham Associates; p. 157 'Romance' by W.J. Turner, used with permission; p. 160 'El Condor Pasa (If I Could)' copyright © English lyrics by Paul Simon 1970, 1997 by Paul Simon Music, Daniel A. Robles and Jorge Milchberg 1933, 1963, 1970 by Edward B. Marks Music Company

Thanks to the following for permission to reproduce photographs and images:

p. 1 Shutterstock/Vinicius Tupinamba; p. 4 M.Sobreira/Alamy; p. 6 Shutterstock/Jeff Banke; p. 17 Shutterstock/Krivosheev Vitaly; p. 23 Lebrecht Music and Arts Photo Library/Alamy; p. 26 Shutterstock/ingret; p. 28 Fabfoodpix.com/Tim Hill © 2002–2011; p. 29 Antony Nettle/Alamy; p. 30 iStockphoto/Thinkstock; p. 32 text and photo from the website of United Colors of Benetton; p. 35 Shutterstock/Pavel Cheiko; p. 36 Shutterstock/stocker1970; p. 37 Mary Grace Long/Asia Images/Corbis; p. 40 Digital Vision/Thinkstock; p. 44 Mary Evans Picture Library/THE WOMEN'S LIBRARY; p. 50 Shutterstock/Karuka; p. 55 iStock/Ralf Hettler; p. 57 Shutterstock/John Dorado; p. 58 Shutterstock/Dennis Donohue; p. 61 Shutterstock/a_v_d; p. 64 Neil Bowman/FLPA; p. 67 Shutterstock/Gail Johnson; p. 73 Moviestore collection Ltd/Alamy; p. 75 Chris Howes/Wild Places Photography/Alamy; p. 84 Shutterstock/AZP Worldwide; p.88 Shutterstock/2happy; p. 91 Philip Pound/Alamy; p. 92*t* Shutterstock/Alexander Chaikin; p. 92*b* Shutterstock/Heiti Paves; p. 96 Photos 12/Alamy; p. 101 Robbie Jack/Corbis; p. 109 Image Source/Alamy; p. 110 Getty Images; p. 114 Stuart Freedman/In Pictures/Corbis; p. 116 Sebastian Kennerknecht/Minden Pictures/FLPA; p. 122 Per Karlsson-BKWine.com/Alamy; p. 127 Shutterstock/kwest; p. 131 Robert Matton AB/Alamy; p. 138 Picture Contact BV/Alamy; p. 142 Shutterstock/J Helgarson; p. 143 bildbroker.de/Alamy; p. 145 F1 ONLINE/SuperStock; p. 147 Brian North Stock Images/Alamy; p. 150 Anna Kern/Etsa/Corbis; p. 154 Mary Evans Picture Library; p. 157 Radius Images/Corbis; p. 159 iStock/oanav; cover Thor Jorgen/Shutterstock